How to Win the Three Games of Golf

Hank Johnson
with Roger Schiffman

GOLF
DIGEST

POCKET BOOKS

New York   London   Toronto   Sydney   Tokyo   Singapore

To the memory of my father and mother, Henry and Helen Johnson, who provided me with more opportunities than any child could imagine. Among the most special of the many gifts was an introduction to the game of golf. I doubt that any parents have ever been more supportive.

To my brother, Steve, whose wisdom and encouragement helped me keep going when it would have been very easy to quit.

And to my wife, Sybil, and my children, Hank, Ashley, Suellen and Michael. Without their friendship and love, nothing that I have accomplished would have any meaning whatsoever.

–H.J.

To Patricia, who gave me the support and encouragement, and Kathleen Manon, who gave me the inspiration.

–R.S.

Published by:

NYT SPECIAL SERVICES, INC.
An Affiliate of The New York Times Company
5520 Park Avenue, Box 395
Trumbull, CT 06611-0395

and

POCKET BOOKS, a division of Simon & Schuster Inc.
1230 Avenue of the Americas
New York, NY 10020

Book Design by Laura Hough

Photography by Jim Moriarty

Illustrations by Elmer Wexler

ISBN: 0-671-86683-4

First NYT Special Services, Inc. and Pocket Books hardcover printing August 1993

10 9 8 7 6 5 4 3 2 1

Printed in the U.S.A.

Contents

Acknowledgments

To properly thank all of the individuals who have contributed to the knowledge from which this book is drawn would take an additional volume of at least equal size.

We are all products of the many pieces of information and experiences we are exposed to, and even if an attempt were made to recognize them all it would probably be incomplete.

I would, however, like to recognize several works and individuals worthy of special mention. In addition to the direct references that are cited throughout the book, works that I have drawn upon and would recommend as resources for serious students of the game are: *The Search for the Perfect Swing* by Alastair Cochran and John Stobbs; *The Golfing Machine* by Homer Kelley and its interpretation by Ben Doyle of Carmel, California, and *Five Lessons: The Modern Fundamentals of Golf* by Ben Hogan. Over the years I have no doubt read well over 100 books on golf and have reviewed all of the significant golf videotapes, all of which have without question influenced my view of the game. That influence is hereby recognized and acknowledged.

Many individuals who have been extremely generous with their time and information over the years have also influenced my development as a golf teacher and coach.

I would also like to offer special thanks to all the great teachers I have had the privilege to work with in the Golf Digest Schools. I sincerely believe that this group collectively represents the most creative and effective array of teachers ever assembled. To this group of very special individuals, especially Bob Toski and the late Davis Love, Jr., I will always be grateful for our association and our common bond through our efforts to help people play better golf.

—*Hank Johnson*

Introduction

How to Win the Three Games of Golf will not give you instant gratification. It is not designed to do so. If you want to cut strokes off your handicap overnight without doing any practice, or learn enough about the game this morning to hack it around on the course this afternoon without going through the process of developing your fundamentals, then go waste your money on some other golf instruction book. This one is not for you. But if you truly want to permanently improve your full-swing and

Hank Johnson

short-game technique, significantly lower your scores over time, and achieve the ultimate joy that only comes from the pursuit of mastery of the game, then invest your money—and your time—in this book.

The unique approach to learning golf that I offer here has helped many of my students. One of them, a neurologist from Montgomery, Ala., was floundering with his golf game. He was a single-digit handicapper who had been a respected tournament player for some 30 years, but his game had slowly deteriorated until finally he couldn't get the ball in the hole at all. The affliction he had on the greens was worse than the yips: He had lost his confidence on long putts as well as short putts. And his lack of conviction with the putter had permeated his full swing. What once was a fun, relaxing game became an embarrassing, painful ordeal. Whenever he played with friends or in a tournament, all he was trying to do was not humiliate himself. Instead of breezing around in the low 70s, he was desperately trying just to finish each hole, in his words, "without something terrible happening."

How did my friend, an intelligent and talented individual, get into such a golfing mess? The answer is that throughout his long struggle, he was often working on the right things in his golf game, but until recently he was going about it in a nonproductive way. He would spend countless hours on the putting green working on his stroke and on the range beating balls, his mind filled with mechanical thoughts. What he needed to do was get on a program where he could work on learning the mechanics of his putting stroke and swing away from those practice balls, so when he did hit balls on the range or played 18 holes his mind could be free of those mechanical thoughts and be focused on performing.

About two years ago, I started him on a unique training program that I am convinced is the quickest and soundest way to really permanently change a faulty golf swing or develop a solid one. This program can be broken down into three distinct areas of the game, which I call (1) the Golf Swing, (2) the Golf Shot and (3) the Golf Score. The training program applies to all aspects of the game, from the shortest putts to the longest drives, and everything in between. Broken down, it looks like this:

THE THREE GAMES OF GOLF

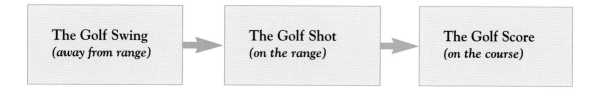

Now all of the doctor's work on the Golf Swing—the mechanics of the motion, from putting to chipping to pitching to the full swing—is done away from the course and away from the practice range or putting green. This is usually at home, in front of a full-length mirror, often without a club and always without a ball.

When he goes to the range, it is merely to work on different shots, to put those mechanics into practice. This is where he learns to shape shots—to hit draws, fades, high shots, low shots. He practices hitting to targets. He develops feel for how far and high the ball travels with different clubs. *When he finds himself thinking of mechanical thoughts, he stops hitting balls* and goes to an area—maybe it's on the back of the range tee—where he can practice those mechanics without the distraction of golf balls. He stays away from the balls until he is comfortable with his mechanics and is refocused on his golf *shots* rather than his golf *swing*. Only then does he go back to his hitting station.

On the course, he thinks solely of making a score, by using those different shots he has practiced. He thinks only of nonmechanical thoughts, such as tempo, strategy and the conditions (wind, firmness of the greens, the lie of the ball).

Once I put him on such a program, mostly for his putting at first, he finally started making some real progress. Last year, he won his club championship by holing nearly every makable putt he looked at. By working on his putting and full swing away from the range and the course, he's now playing good golf again.

But the secret is staying on the program. The funny thing about this neurologist's story—and there is a lesson here for all of us—is that when I first put him on his putting-improvement program I told him he couldn't give up on it without calling me first. After a few weeks, he was fed up and putting worse than ever. I had taken him from 36 putts a round to 40 putts a round. He tried to call me several times to tell me he wanted to abandon the program, but I was traveling a lot and he couldn't get in touch with me for almost five weeks. Out of loyalty, he kept his word and stayed on the program. Before he could give up, he started putting better than ever.

It's like the story Truett Cathy, owner of the vast chain of Chick-Fil-A restaurants, loves to tell about the Chinese bamboo tree. Truett says that you water and fertilize a little seed for a year and nothing happens. You keep watering and fertilizing the seed for the second year and still nothing happens. The same for the third and fourth year. Then early in the fifth year, this plant suddenly grows 90 feet in six weeks. Now the question is, did the Chinese bamboo tree take six weeks to grow, or four-plus years and six weeks? Improving at golf is like that. You could work on a specific mechanical move in your swing for months and you might not experience any improvement. Then almost as if by magic you will be able to do it. You have to have faith in what you're doing and keep at it until it works, no matter how long it takes. You must have the courage to keep on working even when it seems like you are not getting any better. *If you are really committed to being as good as you can be at golf, then understand that there is no finish line.*

Another golfer I know, a woman who is a successful investment broker in Birmingham, started playing golf in high school, gave it up during college, and only a few years ago decided she wanted to play again, well enough to impress the clients she often entertains on the golf course.

She is always looking for the quick fix whenever she misses a couple of greens or a few putts. Instead of seeking a solution to a swing fault that would give her beneficial results over the long term, she opts for some instant cure—a magical swing key—that will work long enough to get her through the next week, the next round, the next hole, the next shot. If that sounds familiar, I'm not surprised.

That seems to be the approach most golfers take today. But that's just the problem. After a while, she has more keys than the security guards at Fort Knox.

It's an easy entanglement to get into, and stems, really, from our modern society in general. Everyone is too busy to make a long-term commitment to improvement. Television and other forms of media tell us we all can expect instant gratification. We microwave our food, blow-dry our hair, skim USA Today and, yes, learn to play golf in a weekend. Sorry, not from me.

Quick fixes may be great if you don't care about ever being really good at golf. But quick fixes in the long run almost always make matters worse. For example, say you have a problem hitting your putts on line. Most of them are finishing to the right of the hole. A friend, trying to be helpful, tells you during a round that you should just aim more to the left. So you try it, and sure enough, you hole your next two five-footers. In fact, you putt fairly well for the rest of the day. But the next day, still aiming left of your target, you notice that most of your putts are again finishing to the right of the hole. What has happened is that you have subconsciously compensated within your stroke for the misalignment at address. You had been pushing your putts within your stroke, and now, by misaligning more to the left, you have made your stroke even more ineffective. The quick fix worked for a while, but now you are worse off than before.

You have two options: You can choose instant gratification and pay long-term consequences or you can put up with temporary inconvenience for permanent improvement. The better solution would be to ask your teacher to check your fundamentals at address—alignment of the put-terface, the position of your eyes over the ball, the square-ness of your grip, arms and feet. Then have your teacher check the path of your stroke and alignment of the blade at impact. You can check these fundamentals at home by placing a mirror on the floor, directly under your eyes. Once you know your fundamentals are correct, you can stroke your putts confidently. It may not happen the next day or the next week, but over the next few weeks your putting should improve significantly and, in general, will continue to be good for as long as you use this practice method.

Golf Should Be No Different from Other Sports

The premise of this book goes right to the heart of our neurologist's and our investment broker's problems. I feel very strongly that you can't efficiently learn to play golf by beating balls on the range or getting caught up in mechanical theory or trying Band-Aid cures. In every other sport, whether it be football, basketball or baseball, first you develop the physical attributes to play the game, then you work on fundamentals with drills, then you practice playing situations by scrimmaging, then you actually play the game. In other sports, 80 to 90 percent of the time is spent in practice and 10 to 20 percent is spent playing the real game. Most golfers do just the opposite.

For example, in basketball, first come the physical attributes—agility, stamina and the ability to jump; then you work on fundamentals—dribbling with both hands, shooting with both hands and knowing all the basic ways to pass the ball, all developed with drills; next, in practice sessions you run through different plays, scrimmaging through fast-breaks and zone or man-to-man defenses, making corrections along the way without worrying about the score; and finally you play a real game of basketball, where you focus only on reacting to the situations that develop with as few thoughts about mechanics as possible.

Why should golf be any different? It shouldn't be. *It can't be.*

That's why I break the game down into three areas, and this book is similarly organized in three parts: (I) the Golf Swing, (II) the Golf Shot and (III) the Golf Score. I see too many people trying to play Golf Swing, when they should be playing Golf Shot or Golf Score. In fact, I believe that 90 percent of all golfers play only Golf Swing. They play Golf Swing on the range, and they play Golf Swing on the course. The game becomes a struggle because all they think about is swing mechanics.

Learning proper swing mechanics is absolutely essential to playing good golf. But you will master those mechanics faster if you work on them without a ball. *Golf is a game of doing something, not simply of knowing something.* If just knowing was enough, then all the teachers could beat all the tour players. Just knowing the information won't help you unless you go through the physical training process and learn to implement it. George H. Sage, in his book *Motor Learning and Control—A Neuropsychological Approach,* defines motor learning as "A relatively permanent change in behavior that is a result of practice and experience." If the change is not relatively permanent, it is not a result of learning, but of some other transient factor, such as having your teacher present while you make swings. It's like the analogy Dr. Richard Schmidt, one of the world's leading experts in motor behavior research, makes so well in his book, *Motor Learning and Performance—From Principles to Practice*:

> When water is heated to a boil, there are changes in its behavior (performance). Of course, these are not permanent because the water returns to the original state as soon as the effects of the [transient factor] (heating) dissipate. These changes therefore would not be parallel to learning changes. However, when an egg is boiled, its state is changed. This change is relatively permanent because cooling the egg does not reverse its state to the original. The changes in the egg are parallel to relatively permanent changes due to learning. When people learn, relatively permanent changes occur that survive the shift to other conditions or the passage of time. After learning, you are not the same person you were before, just as the egg is not the same egg.

To develop a really sound putting stroke, or golf swing, you must make a large number of correct repetitions over a long period of time. The key to practicing effectively is not how many times you do it right, but how few times you do it wrong. Because every time you make an incorrect repetition you back up a little bit. In other words, you make yourself better at doing it wrong. Which is why, when you are working on mechanics, the key is to get yourself in an environment where you can do it correctly over and over and over until that is the natural way you do it without a lot of conscious thought. At that point learning has taken place because in all probability the change in your golf technique will be relatively permanent.

You see, learning the golf swing is learning a highly complex motor skill. Again, according to Schmidt in his book, *Motor Learning and Performance*, "Skill consists in the ability to bring about some end result with maximum certainty. . . . Just because one throws a bull's-eye in darts doesn't mean [he] is a skilled dart player. It means [he] got very lucky on one throw. But [one is] a skilled dart player when [he] can throw bull's-eyes with some degree of certainty. For example, when [he] can produce bull's-eyes reliably on demand without luck playing a very large role." Too many people are on the golf course trying to play golf before they develop the necessary skill. Just because they hit one good drive in their lives means to them that they should always be able to hit a good drive and always hit the driver off the tee. And you hear them say it: "Well, I did it once. I don't understand why I can't do it every time."

The only way to permanently learn a motor skill is through repetition. You simply cannot do it without practice, and lots of it. But it has to be the right kind of practice. And that's what I will stress in the section of this book about swing mechanics. If I've learned anything in my 25 years of teaching golf to players of all levels of ability, it's that it is futile to stand on a practice tee in front of a pile of golf balls and try to learn how to make a good golf swing. That's like putting a person who's on a diet in a roomful of ice cream. It is just not the most productive environment for him or her to be in. I have noticed that without exception my students learn a lot faster if they work on mechanics without the distraction of trying to hit a golf ball at the same time.

You see, most golfers have two conflicting goals when they practice: Performing as well as possible and learning as much as possible. Again, Richard Schmidt:

> The learner who attempts to perform as well as possible (Goal 1) tends to be inhibited from modifying movements from attempt to attempt, which detracts from learning as much as possible (Goal 2). The approach for maximizing performance, repeating the most effective pattern discovered so far, is not effective for learning because it discourages experimentation. Some way to separate the processes inherent in these two goals seems necessary to make learning efficient.

One reason this three-pronged approach works is that it separates learning and performance and makes efficient use of the student's time. You don't have to go to the practice range to work on your swing. In fact, it will be more productive for you not to. For example, I encourage people to work on their mechanics during a break at the office, or in the hotel room when traveling on business. What better way to spend your coffee break than to do a few high-precision practice drills or hone your putting technique and touch?

A constant theme I will be referring to throughout this book is what I've found to be an efficient learning sequence—the **Learning Triangle.** It is based on the countless hours of research I have done at the American Sports Medicine Institute (ASMI) in Birmingham and looks like this:

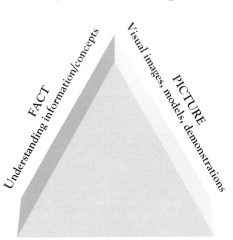

FEEL
Drills, shadowboxing, eyes closed

Most great athletes, from Charles Barkley to Roger Clemens to Bo Jackson, develop the ability to learn by feel because that is the way they have to perform. But the process must go from *fact* to *picture* to *feel*. Let's say you've decided that at address your spine needs to be tipped forward, toward the ball, 45 degrees from vertical. (That's the fact.) The second step in the learning process would be to stand in front of a mirror and practice that dimension of your posture. Study your reflection, making whatever adjustments are necessary for correct posture. (That's the picture.) The third step would be to practice getting into the same posture with your eyes closed and then open them and check your reflection in the mirror. Finally, fix it if it's not correct, then close your eyes again to focus on how it feels when it is correct. (That's the feel.) Now, whatever you are going to learn about the golf swing, that sequence will optimize the process. I will remind you of it constantly throughout Part I.

In this book you will be told how to use various, easy-to-find props to enhance your visual feedback and to develop feel in your swing. Some of the inexpensive items you will need if you want to get the most out of this book:

- ▲ A full-length mirror (not pictured here). If you don't have one, this can be obtained at a home-improvement type of store. It should be at least three feet wide and six feet high.
- ▲ A smaller mirror, 12 x 18 inches, to place flat on the floor.
- ▲ A small kitchen broom, with tape on the handle marking the length of your various clubs, for example, sand wedge and driver.
- ▲ A smaller kitchen broom, about 2-1/2 feet long.
- ▲ A plane board. I will show you how to build a simple one, or have one built.
- ▲ Several cutoff golf shafts, painted bright colors.
- ▲ A carpenter's chalk line.
- ▲ A weighted club. I will tell you how to make or buy one.
- ▲ A standard-size soccer ball.
- ▲ A pair of Ping-Pong paddles.
- ▲ A can of white spray paint.
- ▲ A pair of hinges.
- ▲ Towels, preferably white.
- ▲ Masking tape and electrical tape.
- ▲ A stepladder.

There are other everyday items that you will need, and I will introduce them in subsequent chapters. But for now, if you put yourself on this learning program, and stick with it, I am confident that very soon you will be shooting lower scores, and enjoying the game more.

Most golf instruction is aimed at repairing a person's current swing. That is not the intent of this book. The goal of this book is to provide a program for the development of sound fundamentals. It is designed to help you learn how to swing. This is not a quick-fix book. It is a guide book for your personal golf journey toward permanent improvement. It won't happen overnight, but you will be a much better golfer in the not-too-distant future if you regularly apply the program that follows as it is presented. Good luck and have fun. I'll be pulling for you all along the way.

Part I

The Golf Swing

In this section on developing your Golf *Swing,* everything I instruct you to do can be done—*should be done*—away from the golf course and even away from the practice range. This will separate learning and performance and allow you to be more effective at both. *That is the essence of this book.* I will show you how to improve your swing mechanics, from the tiniest putting stroke to the longest motion with your driving club, by using various drills. But you will experience the fastest improvement if you do these drills most often without a club and always without a ball.

When you are trying to concentrate on learning the various positions of your body and club at address and throughout the swinging motion, the ball only serves as a distraction, because it automatically shifts your focus to performance rather than learning. It is difficult to concentrate on making a mechanically correct swing and hit the ball at the same time. When you are making a practice swing, you are learning. When you are hitting a golf shot, you are performing. My research, as previously stated, indicates that when you try to learn and perform at the same time you usually do a lousy job of both. So, *you will not be hitting balls when working on learning the mechanics of your swing.* Conversely, you will not be working on mechanics when you are actually hitting balls at the range and on the course as outlined in other sections of this book.

All the drills in this section are designed to be done at home, in the office, in the locker room. When you are executing these drills, remember the Learning Triangle discussed in the introduction to the book. First, understand the correct positions and motions. Second, create some kind of visual feedback to check those positions and motions (looking in a mirror, for example). Third, learn to feel those positions and motions (closing your eyes while executing the drill).

If you are on the practice range and find yourself thinking about swing mechanics, the best thing to do is muster up whatever discipline it takes and get away from your hitting area. Go to the back of the range, away from that pile of practice balls. There you can make as many rehearsal swings as you like, concentrating on permanently learning proper swing mechanics.

There are two types of practice—blocked practice and random practice. Blocked practice is when you are doing the same thing over and over, as in executing the many repetitions necessary to develop sound swing mechanics as a physical habit. You are trying to create a large number of correct repetitions with a minimum number of incorrect repetitions. Random practice is when you change one of the parameters—maybe it's your target, maybe it's your club, for example—which is what you should do when learning shots on the range. Both types of practice are valid, but blocked practice is what you will be doing in this section on the mechanics of the Golf Swing. That is why I want you to be in an environment where you can repeat various correct swing positions and motions over and over and over until they are permanently learned.

Whether you are putting, chipping, pitching or making full swings, the basic motion can be broken down into three areas: (1) the pivot, (2) the arms and (3) the hands/wrists. This section on the Golf Swing comprises three such chapters, beginning with the pivot.

1 | The Pivot

When I begin working with a student for the first time, I usually ask a number of basic questions: One is, "Which part of the body should the arms, shoulders and club rotate around during the swing?" Almost to a person, the response is "the head." Some pupils might say something similar, like "the chin." But the general belief is that the head should serve as the axis around which the rest of the body should turn and the club should swing. That thinking results in part from the tremendous quantity

of instruction that advocates keeping the head "still." Taken literally, it is dead wrong, and can kill a potentially great golf swing.

While the head shouldn't slide much to the right on the backswing, it should, however, *rotate* to the right, around the spine. So the pivot motion is the rotation of the shoulders about a fixed point, which should be the top of the spine. That shoulder rotation is always perpendicular to the spine (see Photo 1). Because the spine in the golf swing is tipped forward toward the ball, at the end of the backward portion of the pivot, the left shoulder is lower than the right. At the end of the forward portion of the

pivot, the right shoulder is lower than the left (see Photo 2). After studying hundreds of photographs of all the great players throughout the history of the game, I have concluded that in every effective swing *the head also rotates* around the top of the spine. Anything less results in a reverse tilt of the spine (toward the target) at the top of the backswing and a reverse weight shift (moving to the left side on the backswing, then the right side on the downswing), which leads to a loss of distance and diminished accuracy. Before I get into further detail about the pivot, you need to understand proper posture and how to create a consistent address routine.

First, Use a Wall to Create the Proper Full-swing Posture

Photo 1: Stand with your hips against a wall, your heels three to four inches away from it.

Photo 2: Keeping your back straight so you are leaning against the wall with the top half of your body, slide your hips down the wall two or three inches by bending your knees out over the balls of your feet. This gives you the proper knee flex.

Photo 3: Next, simply tip your spine forward from the hips, keeping your back relatively straight until the fronts of your shoulders are over your toes. This gives you the right amount of spine angle toward the ball.

Not only does this drill help you develop perfect posture for your swing, it gives you a sense of how the top of your spine is the fixed pivot point for your shoulders to rotate around. I often have my students do 20 repetitions of this drill twice a day until this posture position becomes natural and doesn't require any conscious thought.

1   2   3

Next, Develop a Consistent Address Routine

The pivot motion in the golf swing creates energy. It is what drives all the other movements. But before you can begin to learn the proper pivot motion, it is essential that you establish a repeatable address routine. You need to set up exactly the same way every time to be sure of such factors as alignment, ball position and posture. Once you have mastered this preswing routine—at home and without a ball—the pivot motion will be much easier.

First, place two pieces of tape in a "T" configuration on the floor, as shown in the photo below. Where the two pieces of tape intersect indicates the ball position. The shorter piece of tape indicates the impact line. The longer piece of tape indicates the target line. Now, keeping in mind the posture you learned in the previous drill, the address routine you should rehearse is a three-step process and should always be performed exactly in this order:

1. Determine the impact line with the inside of your right foot. (If you had a putter or other club in your hand you also would be aiming the face down the target line at this time.)

2. Step over the impact line with your left foot and establish your ball position (though you have no ball) with your left heel—two inches inside your left heel for a shot from the ground, opposite your left heel for a shot from a tee.

3. Drop your right foot back to create your final stance width and alignment. You should repeat this routine at home daily, over and over, until it becomes automatic. On the golf course you don't want to have to think about it.

A Closer Look at the Pivot

Keeping your address routine in mind, there are two basic pivot motions: one for putting and chipping; one for all the other strokes, from pitching to full shots with the driver. The principles of the pivot are basically the same, the only difference is the size and speed of the motion. You increase the size and speed of the pivot by the way the rest of your body responds to it. The putting and chipping pivot has a motionless lower body. The pivot for the other strokes uses the lower body to add thrust to the movement of the shoulders, which in turn adds thrust to the arms, which in turn adds thrust to the club.

Putting and chipping pivot   *Pitch-and-run pivot*

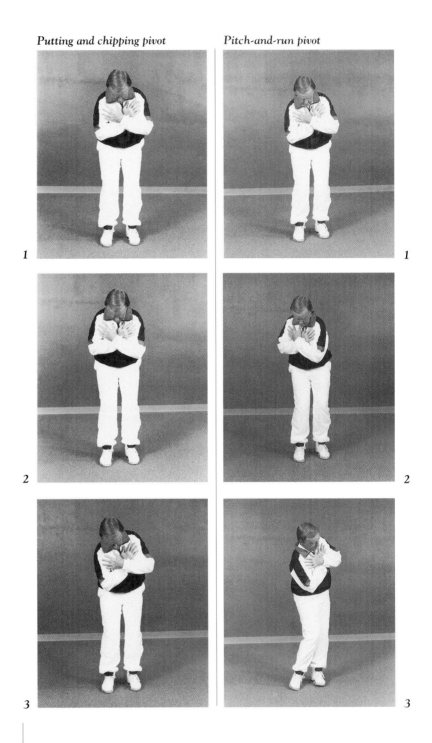

1

1

2

2

3

3

1   1

2   2

3   3

Putting Pivot

Because in putting the spine is tilted more toward the ball than in all the other strokes, the plane of the shoulder rotation is more vertical. So the pivot motion for putting involves a rocking of the shoulders about the top of the spine. The left shoulder moves down to swing the hands and arms back, then it moves up to swing them through.

Not too long ago, the neurologist I mentioned in the introduction had completely lost confidence in his putting stroke. He was three-putting several times every round and a four-putt was not uncommon. The first thing I did was put him on a program away from the practice green where he could work simply on the mechanics and feel of a correct stroke, and that began with the pivot. To get the feel of the proper pivot in the putting motion, I had the doctor perform the Doorjamb Drill about 20 times a day. It worked wonders for his basic stroke. Here's how to do it:

Learn Putting Pivot
with the Doorjamb Drill

This drill will teach you the feeling of the putting pivot, which comes entirely from the movement of the shoulders. Your body should stay relatively quiet throughout the putting motion.

1

Photo 1: Without a putter, position yourself so your left hip is against the side of a doorjamb. Your feet should be about 12 inches apart, your left foot square but pulled back from the target line so it is 10 degrees open to it. The open stance promotes keeping your lower body motionless and restricts hip rotation, critical to a repeating putting stroke. The left toe should be about 12 inches from where the ball would be. Tip your spine forward until your eyes are directly over that imaginary ball. Put the backs of your hands together with the right wrist under the left. Your elbows should have about 45 degrees of bend in them.

2

Photo 2: *Concentrate on swinging your arms and hands by moving your shoulders.* The left shoulder goes down to move the arms and hands back.

Photo 3: The left shoulder goes up to move the arms and hands through. The doorjamb against your left hip should restrict your lower body so it can't move while your arms and hands swing through.

▲ **Remember the Learning Triangle:** First repeat this motion several times, looking at the position of your arms and shoulders throughout your stroke. Then practice the motion a few times with your eyes closed. Concentrate on how the movement feels.

3

Learn Putting Setup
with a Mirror on the Floor

I also gave the doctor a simple drill to help align his eyes correctly over the ball. If your eyes are in a different position each time you stand over a putt, you will see a different picture. I was convinced that the reason he had such difficulty putting is that he never got his eyes in the same place two days in a row. All it required was a simple 12- x 18-inch mirror and some masking tape. He practiced with this device about five minutes every evening until a proper putting address position became automatic. Here's how to do it:

Photo 1: Place a strip of masking tape lengthwise on the reflective side of the mirror.

Photo 2: Then place another strip of tape perpendicular to the first strip. Place the mirror on the floor. The point where the two strips of tape intersect is where the ball would be, but don't use a ball yet.

Photo 3: With your putter, line up to that imaginary ball, the putterblade aligned with the cross section of tape. The reflection of your eyes should be just behind the ball and exactly on the lengthwise tape, which is also your target line. Practice getting into this address position several times, until it feels comfortable, always making sure your eyes are directly on that target line. Now, make some practice strokes with the same motion you learned in the Doorjamb Drill, using your shoulders to make the pivot. Your putter should track back and forth along the target line. It's OK if your putter swings slightly inside to along to

1

2

3

back inside that line. But if it swings outside that line, adjust accordingly.

Practice setting up to your mirror 10 to 20 times each evening. If you want, you can place a ball at the intersection of the two pieces of tape while you practice your stroke. Your putting setup and stroke should improve dramatically over time.

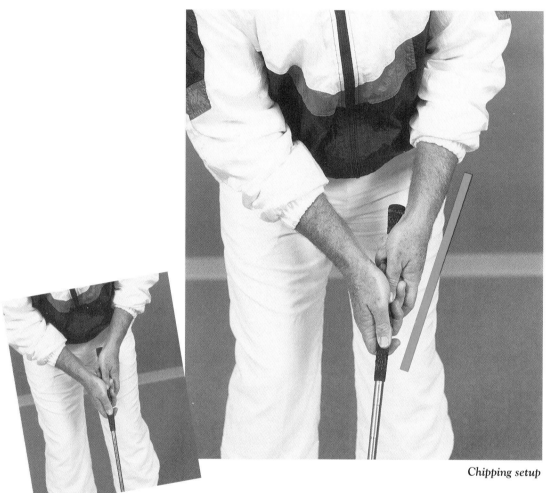

Chipping setup

Putting setup

Chipping Pivot

The chipping pivot is the same as the putting pivot. The only variables that change are the loft of the club and the address position of the shaft. In the chipping setup the ball position is the same as for putting—off the left heel for a right-hander—unless the ball is not sitting cleanly. Then the ball should be positioned nearer the center of your stance (to the right for a right-hander). Lean the clubshaft forward (toward the target) until your left wrist is flat. After that, the pivot motion is the same—left shoulder down to swing the hands and arms back; left shoulder up to swing the hands and arms through.

Lean Shaft Against Left Hip to Learn Chipping Pivot

As in the putting pivot, your lower body should remain quiet in the chipping pivot. To promote a stable lower body, without a club in your hand make a few chipping motions while a club is propped against your left hip. Place the club so the clubhead is on the ground or floor and the grip is resting against the side of your hip (see photo). You'll know if your lower body moved during the chipping motion if the club fell during your stroke.

1   2   3

Pitching Pivot

The pivot for the basic pitching motion contains a bit more lower-body thrust than does the motion for putting and chipping. Your weight is evenly balanced on both feet with your stance line (across your toes) 20 degrees open to the target line. Photo 1: As the left shoulder moves down to perform the backswing pivot, the lower-body momentum causes the hips to rotate and the weight to move toward the right heel. Photo 2: Then coming through the hips turn back toward the target and the weight moves toward the left heel. So, the left shoulder goes down and up. The weight goes right heel, left heel. Photo 3: The right shoulder should be lower than the left at the finish, the right knee coming over to the left.

Practice with Arms Crossed
to Learn Full-length Pitching Pivot

Pitch shots vary in length from about 20 yards to the distance of your full wedge. The farther you are going to hit the ball, the bigger pivot you need. You can learn the overall pitching pivot by performing this drill in front of a full-length mirror.

Photo 1: With your stance line (the line across your toes) about 20 degrees open to an imaginary target, first set up to an imaginary ball with your arms crossed.

Photo 2: Next, for a full-length pitch, turn your hips and shoulders *together* to the right until your left shoulder is directly over the instep of your right foot. Your left heel should not come off the ground.

Photo 3: Finally, turn your hips and shoulders *together* back to the left until your right knee touches your left knee. Your right shoulder should remain lower than your left at the finish. This is a motion you are going to build on for the full swing, so it is very important to practice it over and over until your positions naturally match mine.

▲ **Remember the Learning Triangle:** Do the drill a few times while looking at your reflection in the mirror and checking each of your positions. Then do it a couple of times with your eyes closed until you can feel your weight shifting properly to your right heel going back, then to the outside of your left foot coming through and around to your left heel for the finish. At the finish your knees should be touching, your left leg straight and your right shoulder lower than your left.

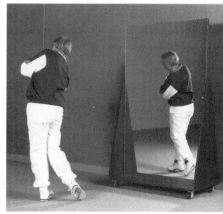

1

2

3

Full-swing Pivot

Compared with the pitching pivot, the pivot motion for full swings has one key difference, and that relates to the first move down from the top of the swing, which creates "elastic loading" throughout the body. Think of the full-swing pivot as a count of 1-2-3. The shoulders turn, hold and unturn. The hips turn, shift and unturn. So that means while the shoulders are holding, the hips are shifting toward the target. That allows the hips to lead on the downswing. The holding of the shoulders at the top gives the hips time to shift and, in effect, the hip shift puts the left leg back where it was at address. On the full-swing pivot, the left shoulder needs to turn back until it is behind your left hip, without any loss of the spine angle that was set up at address. I prefer that the left heel stay on the ground throughout the swing, unless it is pulled up by the pivot.

Hold Broom Across Shoulders to Learn Full-swing Pivot

To quickly gain the feel for the full-swing pivot, try this drill. *Address:* As with the pitching pivot drill, set up to an imaginary ball, again in front of a full-length mirror, but this time holding a broom across your shoulders and behind your neck. With your back relatively straight and your feet square to your target line, bend from the hips until your back is at a 45-degree angle from vertical. (This would be about right for your 5-iron, 40 degrees for your driver, 50 degrees for the 9-iron.) An imaginary ball would be two inches inside your left heel,

Check in the mirror

Close your eyes

Focus on feel

and the right end of the broom should be slightly lower than the left.

Count One: Looking in the mirror and keeping your left heel on the ground, turn back so that at the top your left shoulder moves to the right of your left hip. Count Two: Hold your shoulders turned as you move your left leg and knee back to their address position. Count Three: Then turn through to a full, balanced finish position. Your right shoulder should be lower than the left, the right end of the broom should be closer to the target than the left, your left leg should be straight, your knees together.

Remember the Learning Triangle: First perform this motion looking in the mirror until it is similar to my positions. Then try it with your eyes closed until you can feel the correct positions. Then open your eyes and check those positions in the mirror. Make whatever adjustments are necessary and close your eyes again to focus on how it feels. Go slowly until you are comfortable with each position.

Count 1

Count 2

Address

Count 3

2 | The Arms

It is the responsibility of the pivot to create energy; it is the engine of your swing and does all the work. It is the responsibility of the arms to transfer that energy through the hands into the clubshaft. The left arm produces the swing and maintains its radius. The right arm provides support for the left arm. *One of the fundamental skills that a golfer has to develop to play golf is the ability to straighten the right arm at the elbow without straightening it at the wrist.* The place to start learning how to do that is in the putting and chipping motion.

Practice with Left Arm Behind Back to Learn Right-arm Thrust in Putting and Chipping

In putting and chipping we will train the right arm first, with the following drill. Photo 1: Without a club, set up in the proper putting address position you learned in Chapter 1, and put your left hand behind your back. Put your right arm in front of your body with the palm of your right hand vertical to the ground and your right wrist bent. Photos 2 and 3: Now swing your right arm back and through so the elbow straightens through the impact area while your right wrist stays bent.

1

Remember the Learning Triangle: Watch your right arm as it moves to the right, then back to the left through the impact area, past the left thigh, making sure the elbow straightens and the wrist stays bent. Now do it with your eyes closed, concentrating on feeling your elbow straighten. Open your eyes on your follow-through. If you have straightened your right wrist, adjust it accordingly, close your eyes, and repeat the motion until you can do it correctly every time.

2

3

The Arms

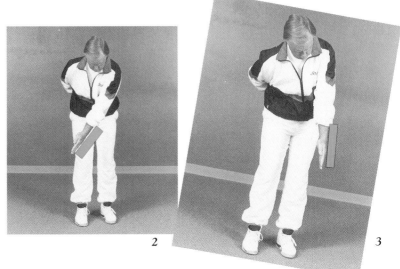

1   2   3

Practice with Right Arm Behind Back to Learn to Keep Left Wrist Flat in Putting and Chipping

The job of the left arm is to be swung from the shoulder by the pivot without the left wrist bending (the back of the hand should stay in line with the back of the forearm).

Photo 1: Set up as in the previous drill, but this time with your right arm behind your back. Photos 2 and 3: With your left palm in front of your body and vertical, swing back and through to the finish without letting your left wrist bend.

Remember the Learning Triangle: Again, repeat this drill several times watching your left arm swing back and through. Then repeat the motion with your eyes closed to learn how your left wrist should feel at the finish. If, when you open your eyes, your left wrist has bent, adjust it accordingly, and repeat the motion with your eyes closed.

Practice Putting/Chipping Arm Swing with the Combination Drill

Photo 1: Finally, place the backs of your hands against each other, the right wrist under the left, as in the Doorjamb Drill. Your right wrist should be bent and your left wrist flat (again, the back of the hand in line with the back of the forearm). Now swing your arms back and through.

Photo 2: Concentrate on straightening your right elbow through the impact area while keeping your right wrist bent and your left wrist flat. Even though your arms are swinging, the movement is coming from your shoulders because they are being moved by the pivot.

1

▲ **Remember the Learning Triangle:** Try it first looking in a mirror to be sure your positions are correct, then with your eyes closed to learn how the motion should feel.

Use a Mirror on Floor to Perfect Putting and Chipping Arm Movement

To check the alignment of your forearms for the putting and chipping motion, practice the Combination Drill over the same T-station mirror you used in the drill for learning the putting pivot. Look at the reflection of your elbows. Make sure they are aligned with the bottom edge of the mirror at address. If they are not, adjust accordingly and make a few strokes. Drill yourself on setting up to the T-station until your forearms are aligned correctly every time. Soon, this will become automatic.

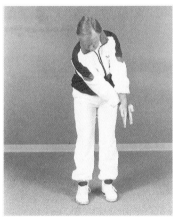

2

The Role of the Arms in Pitching

As the size of the pivot motion increases, there needs to be proportionately more movement of the arms. Everything should move back and through together, nothing independent of anything else. The role of the left arm is still to maintain the radius of the swing. The role of the right arm is still to support the left. As the pivot motion increases for longer shots, the bend in the right elbow increases on the backswing. The role of the right arm on the forward swing is still to straighten at the elbow without the wrist straightening.

To learn the correct function of the arms in the pitching motion, first get into the setup position you practiced for the pitching pivot—feet aligned about 20 degrees open to the target line.

Photo 1: Hold your right wrist with your left hand, your left index finger running along the lifeline of your right hand.

1

2

Practice with your

eyes closed

Check position

Make adjustments

3

Photo 2: On the backswing, allow your right elbow to bend.

Photo 3: On the through-swing, your right elbow should straighten through impact while your right wrist remains bent. You can push back with your left index finger to keep the right wrist bent through impact.

Photo 4: At the finish, your arms should be relaxed and in front of your body, your knees should be together with your left leg straight and your right shoulder should be lower than your left.

▲ **Remember the Learning Triangle:** Practice this pitching motion in front of a full-length mirror until you think you have mastered these positions. Then try it a few times with your eyes closed to ingrain the feeling of those positions. When you open your eyes check to see that you are indeed in the correct positions—on the backswing, right wrist bending; at impact, right elbow straightening with the right wrist bent; at the finish, arms relaxed and in front of your body, knees together and right shoulder lower than the left. Make whatever adjustments are necessary and repeat.

Master positions

Ingrain feel

Adjust and repeat

Hold a Soccer Ball to Learn Role of Arms in the Full Swing

Photo 1: While assuming the proper full-swing address position you learned for the full-swing pivot—feet aligned parallel left of your target line, your back relatively straight, bending from the hips about 45 degrees from vertical—hold a soccer ball, basketball or small beach ball with both hands.

Photo 2: Swing the ball over your right shoulder as you make your backswing pivot. Your left shoulder should move to the right of your left hip on the backswing.

Photo 3: Then swing the ball over your left shoulder as you make your forward-swing pivot, your right shoulder finishing lower and closer to the target than your left shoulder. Do not swing your arms without making the pivot motion. Everything must move back together and through together.

1

▲ **Remember the Learning Triangle:** Practice the Soccer Ball Drill in front of a full-length mirror until you are getting into the proper positions. Then repeat the motion with your eyes closed to learn how those positions feel. Open your eyes to check them in the mirror, adjust accordingly, and repeat.

The Arms

3 | Hands and Wrists

In the previous two chapters we have talked about the pivot creating energy in the swing and the arms transferring that energy into the clubshaft. Now the role of the hands is to be the link between the arms and the club. The hands control the application of energy. They sense and monitor the club. Though the hands must work together in the swing, the flat left wrist, left forearm and hand (for a right-handed player) turn and roll to maintain a square face alignment of the club, and the right hand controls the clubhead mass or weight.

The first joint of the index finger of the right hand, through control of the clubshaft, should sense the mass of the clubhead's weight coming down into the ball and whether or not the clubhead is lagging behind the hands, as it should. In a proper swing, the clubhead should be lagging or following the clubshaft. If not, then most of the club-head energy will have been thrown away before impact. You want to get through impact while that energy is still stored in the clubshaft. That is why it is important to get your hands through the shot with the right wrist still bent.

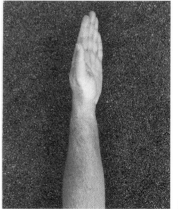

You should assign the responsibility for controlling the clubface to your left hand and for the clubhead and shaft to your right hand. One of the reasons that clubhead "throwaway" (a premature uncocking of the wrists on the downswing) occurs is that a golfer tries to square the face with the right wrist. He or she has taken the left hand's re-sponsibility away from it and assigned it to the wrong hand. *To become an accomplished player, you have to learn to square the face with the rolling of your left hand and forearm and straightening of your right elbow without losing the bend in the back of your right wrist.*

The left *wrist* cocks at the base of the thumb, and the left *hand* and wrist turn and roll. Because of rotation in the left arm, primarily the left forearm, the left hand and wrist turn going back (the palm turns down); they roll go-ing forward (the back of the hand turns down). If we con-sider vertical to the ground as zero (Photo 1), then in a full swing the left hand turns about 45 degrees from vertical to the ground going back (Photo 2) and rolls 90 degrees or about 45 degrees from vertical to the ground going through the ball to the finish (Photo 3). For a square clubface, the

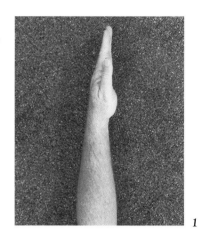

left hand and wrist should be vertical to the ground through impact. If they have not reached vertical, the clubface will be open. If they have rolled past vertical, the clubface will be closed. We will examine this in more detail with some specific drills, but first, let's discuss the proper way to grip the club.

How to Hold the Club for Putting and Chipping

The grip is essentially the same for putting and chipping. It is designed to minimize most wrist movement throughout the stroke. In establishing a putting or chipping grip, place the right hand on the club first.

Photo 1: Put the thumb and thumb pad of the right hand on the top of the grip so the clubshaft runs along the lifeline of your hand.

Photo 2: Then fit the left hand on the club with the left thumb and thumb pad down the top of the grip and

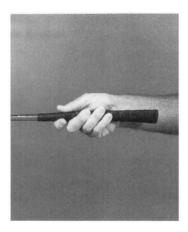
1

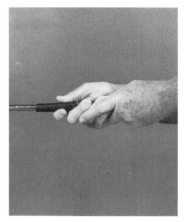
2

3

the clubshaft along the lifeline of your left hand. Do this without moving the right hand any more than you have to. You might want to allow your left index finger to rest on the outside of your right-hand fingers (called a reverse-overlap grip).

Photo 3: What is important, however, is that the clubshaft sits in the palms of both hands and that it is on the same plane as your forearms. For chipping (inset), you will lean your hands toward the target at address until your left wrist is flat (the back of the hand and forearm in line).

Hands and Wrists

1   2   3

How to Hold the Club for Full-swing Shots

The full-swing grip—used for all shots from short pitches on up to the driver—is designed to allow your left wrist to hinge and your right wrist to bend.

Photo 1: First, with the clubhead resting on the ground and your left arm hanging naturally to the left of your left hip, place your left hand on the grip.

Photos 2 and 3: The butt of the club should be placed *under the heel pad of the left hand* to form the left wrist hinge. The thumb should rest slightly to the right of the top of the shaft. There should be no gap between the thumb and the index finger. Tom Kite likes to practice holding a coin there. If it falls out, he has a gap. The pressure points should be under the nails of the last three fingers of your left hand, where the fingers are against the back of the shaft.

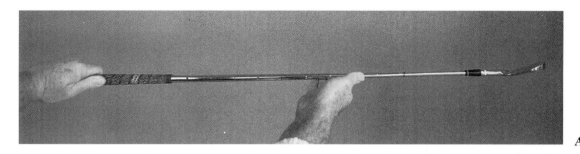

A

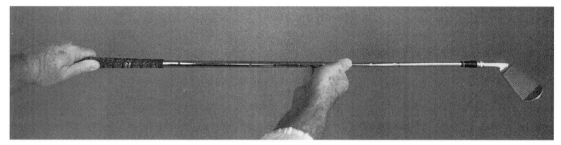

B

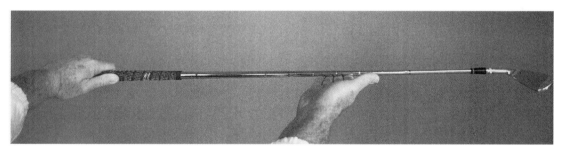

C

You can check your left-hand grip by holding the club horizontally in front of you and flattening your left wrist so the back of your left hand and forearm are parallel to the ground. Photo A: If the clubface is toe-up, your left-hand grip is too strong (too far to the right on the club). Photo B: If the clubface is toe-down, your left-hand grip is too weak (too far to the left). Photo C: If the clubface is horizontal, your left hand is correctly positioned. *Remember: Butt of the club under the heel pad, thumb just to the right of the top of the shaft, no gap.*

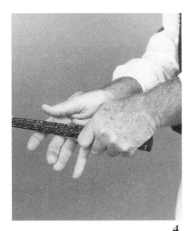

4   5   6

To put the right hand on the club, bring the club up in front of you with your left wrist flat, the clubshaft horizontal to the ground and the leading edge of the clubface vertical to the ground.

Photo 4: Place the palm of your right hand over the left thumb, the first joint of your right index finger against the back of the clubshaft. Again, there should be no gap between the right thumb and the right index finger. Try Tom Kite's coin test. Photos 5 and 6: Continue to lay the other fingers of your right hand on the grip, your right little finger over your left index finger. You may wish to have your right little finger in contact with the club (called a 10-finger grip), or interlock it with the left index finger. This makes little difference, as long as the pressure points are (1) the last three fingers of the left hand against the back of the shaft, (2) the palm of the right hand where it touches the left thumb and (3) the first joint of the right index finger against the back of the shaft.

Use the Ball-dragging Drill to Train Each Hand and Wrist

Photo 1: Gripping your pitching wedge as outlined earlier for a full-swing shot, set up to a ball as if you were going to hit a pitch shot, then take your right hand off the club.

Photo 2: Now start walking toward the target, dragging the ball along the ground with your clubhead. You must keep the clubface square to the target line, the grip end of the shaft leaning forward (toward the target) and your body rotated to the left to hold the ball against the club as you walk.

Photo 3: Now, perform the same motion, but with your left hand off the club. You'll notice that whichever hand is still on the club, that wrist will move into a perfect impact position. If it's the right wrist, it will be bent. If it's the left wrist, it will be flat.

▲ **Remember the Learning Triangle:** With each hand, stop for a moment, close your eyes and concentrate on how each wrist feels. Then open your eyes and continue walking. Once you can do it correctly with each hand separately, try it with both hands.

1

2

3

Understanding the Hinging Action
in Your Swing

In the next few pages I will show you how to use—and even build—a plane board, but first it is helpful to understand how your left shoulder and your left wrist work in the swing, because they are essential to keeping your clubshaft on plane and your clubface square. Think of them as

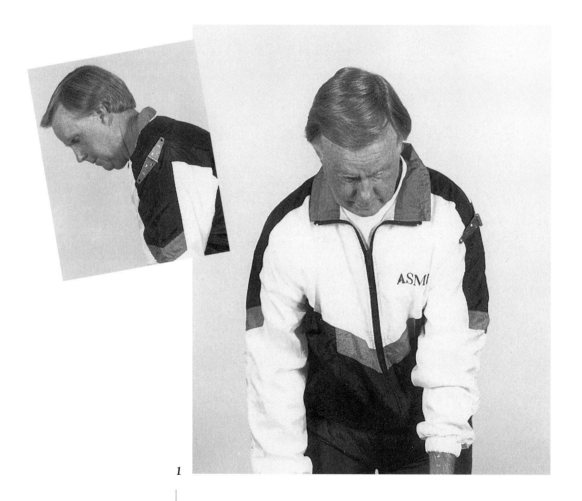

1

hinges. In fact, I'll demonstrate using real hinges and a small broom against the plane board.

Photo 1: During the golf swing the golfer's left shoulder has a hinge pin that is perpendicular to the swing plane (inset), which allows the left arm to swing back and through parallel to the plane.

Photo 2: The left wrist also forms a hinge. Its hinge pin is parallel to the plane (inset) and its function is per-

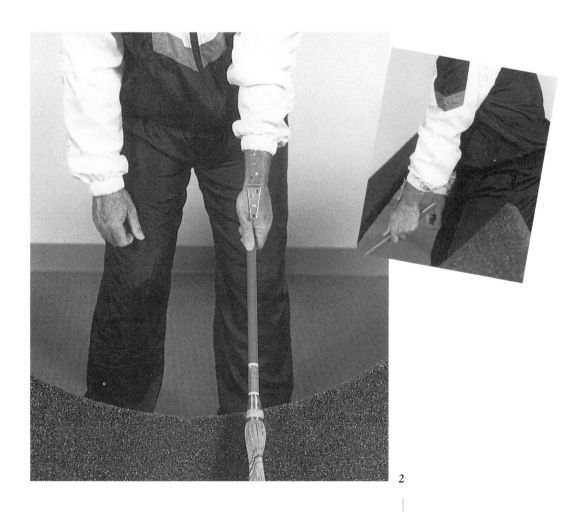

2

pendicular to the plane. That means these hinges at address are not aligned with each other. But between those hinges is a swivel (the left arm). It has the ability to rotate and to keep those hinges properly aligned so the wrist cock and the left arm movement are on the same plane.

Photo 3: As the swing begins, the rotation of the body moves this hinge assembly back. There is no change in their alignment until the broom (or the club) approaches waist high. Then the swivel (the left arm) between the hinges rotates and it turns the left wrist hinge into a position so that the left wrist can cock on plane.

Photos 4 and 5: At this portion of the swing, halfway back on up to the top, the hinge pins would be aligned with each other and the hinges at the wrist and shoulder can function on the same plane.

Photo 6: Coming back down, the wrist unhinges and rolls into its impact position, which is again perpendicular to the plane.

Photo 7: On the forward swing, the swivel (the left arm) allows the wrist to continue to roll until the hinge

3

4

5

6

7

pins would be realigned with each other so the wrist can hinge up the plane for the finish. This is a full-roll motion, which puts the flat left wrist horizontal to the plane for the finish. The full-roll hinge results for most players in a straight or right-to-left ball flight.

Photo 7-A: A reverse roll. Everything is the same back and through along the plane to impact. But at impact the wrist stops turning and continues up the plane as the hinge pin in the left wrist stays parallel to the plane. The

7-A

wrist function is perpendicular to the plane. That requires some other compensation on the left side of the body—the left elbow starts to give way into what's often called the "chicken wing" look. The reverse-roll hinge results in a left-to-right, higher ball flight, which is ideal for a high, soft, cut shot.

Photo 7-B: In between is a half-roll. Again, everything is the same until impact. Then the hinge pin in the wrist continues to roll until it is perpendicular to the ground—but neither parallel nor perpendicular to the plane—for the finish of the swing. The half-roll hinge will create a fade for most players.

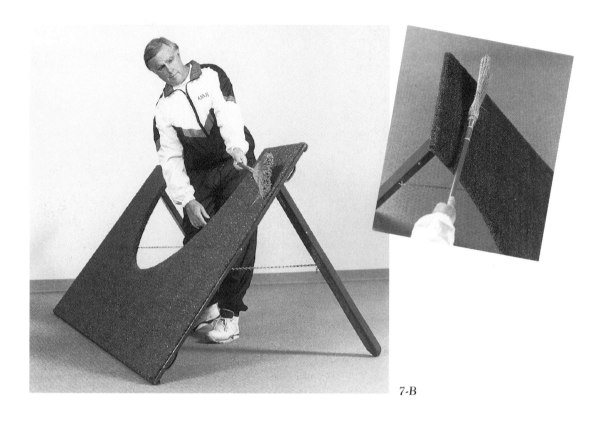

7-B

Building a Weighted Club

Take an old club, either a driver or a 5-iron, and wrap lead tape in barber-pole fashion up the entire shaft, from just under the grip all the way to the hosel or whipping. Then wrap several layers of tape around the clubhead. Distribute the wraps evenly across the top and back of a wood, or across the back of an iron. You may also want to remove the existing grip, pour sand down the shaft, and then install a new grip, being sure to then plug the hole in the butt end with rubber cement or plastic tape.

You can often buy lead tape from a club professional, who can order some for you. You can order lead tape direct from The Golfworks, (4820 Jacksontown Road, Newark, OH 43055, 800-848-8358). It usually costs about $2^{75} for a 100-inch x 1/2-inch wide spool. The Jerry Barber Golden-touch Golf Company makes a weighted practice club (P.O. Box 1687, San Marcos, CA 92079, 800-423-2220). The retail price is about $60^{00}.

Building a Plane Board

Making a plane board is easier than you might think. Give these plans to a carpenter, or build one yourself. All you need is a 4' x 8' sheet of 1/2-inch plywood, two 2 x 4's, a jig saw, carpet, two hinges, 4 eye hooks, thin chain and four handles.

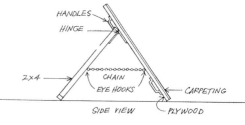

HANDLES
HINGE
2X4
CHAIN
EYE HOOKS
CARPETING
SIDE VIEW
PLYWOOD

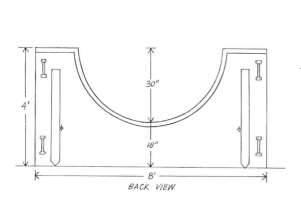

4'
30"
18"
8'
BACK VIEW

Training with a Weighted Club

If you want to train on the plane board with a weighted club, you need to break the swing down into two areas: (1) from the address position to the top, and (2) from just prior to impact through the finish. But you do not need to make a complete full swing along the plane board.

1

Plane Board Drill No. 1: Perfecting Your Backswing

Photo 1: First, set the angle of the plane board so it matches the angle of your clubshaft at address.

Photos 2 and 3: From your address position, swing the weighted club to the top, letting the plane board guide your takeaway. The clubshaft should lightly touch the carpet on the board throughout. When the club points to the back-bottom corner of the plane board, check that the only hinging that has occurred is at the left shoulder. At the top, let the weighted club train the muscles in your arms and hands to hold the club at that point.

2

▲ **Remember the Learning Triangle:** Repeat this backswing motion several times, first with your eyes open, to be sure the clubshaft stays in contact with the plane board. Then make a few backswings with your eyes closed to enhance the feeling of the proper backswing.

3

1   2   3

Plane Board Drill No. 2:
Perfecting Impact and Your Finish

Photo 1: Going forward, point the club at the back-bottom corner of the plane board and turn your hips into a slightly open position that simulates coming into impact.

Photos 2 and 3: Then rotate from there to the finish of the swing. Let the weight of the club, once it's moving up the plane board, pull you into your finish position. Again, the full length of the clubshaft should remain in light contact with the carpet on the plane board.

Again, remember the Learning Triangle: Practice the drill first with your eyes open, to be sure the club is getting into the proper positions. Then repeat with your eyes closed to ingrain the feel of the club following through on a proper plane into the correct finish position.

Practice with

eyes open

Close your eyes

Feel the

proper plane

1

2

3

4

Plane Board Drill No. 3:
Learn the Basic Swing Positions

Swinging a normal club along the plane board is an excellent method for learning where the club should be in several key positions. Study these pictures and try to imitate them.

Photo 1: Set the plane board so it matches the angle of the clubshaft at address when the club is soled properly.

Photo 2: When the club has moved 45 degrees into the backswing (pointing at the bottom-back corner of the plane board), there should be no movement in the swivel (the left arm), the clubface still perpendicular to the plane.

Photo 3: At the waist-high position of the backswing, the swivel begins to operate so the toe of the club rolls up and the face of the club is perpendicular to the ground (angled to the plane).

Photo 4: The swivel continues to roll so the face gets parallel to the plane at the top of the swing. The face and the back of the left arm are aligned with each other.

Photo 5: On the downswing, at the waist-high position, the clubface again is perpendicular to the ground.

Photo 6: The clubface rolls back into its perpendicular-to-the-plane position at impact.

Photo 7: Going through, the clubshaft is now pointed at the bottom-front corner of the plane board and the face is still perpendicular to the plane.

Photo 8: The swivel reacts and rolls. For a full-roll hinge, using a flat left wrist the face rolls onto the plane for the finish of the swing.

Make sure the clubshaft stays lightly in touch with the plane board

▲ **Remember the Learning Triangle:** Repeat this swinging motion with a club several times, first with your eyes open, making sure the full length of clubshaft stays lightly in touch with the plane board. Then make some slow swings with your eyes closed to enhance the feeling of an on-plane swing.

5

6

7

8

1

2

Ping-Pong Paddles Teach Hand and Wrist Control Through Impact

Photo 1: To demonstrate how the hands and wrists control the alignment of the clubface, hold a Ping-Pong paddle in each hand , the paddle blades vertical to the floor.

Photo 2: For a *full roll* of the wrists for the finish and a closing clubface at impact, the paddles when they are hip high need to be turned past vertical until they are about 45 degrees to the floor with the left wrist flat and the right wrist bent. That motion produces a draw for most players.

Photo 3: For a *half roll* of the wrists and a slightly open clubface at impact, the flat left wrist is vertical to the ground as it goes through impact and stays vertical to the ground for the finish. That produces a fade.

Photo 4: For a *reverse roll* of the wrists and an open clubface through impact, the flat left wrist stays vertical to the swing plane or 45 degrees to the ground, in the opposite direction as the full roll, well into the finish. That's useful for cut shots with your wedge or sand wedge, or any shot where you need to hit the ball high and let it move to the right.

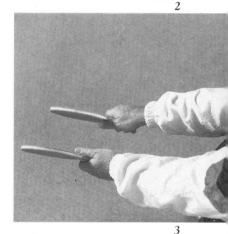

3

4

Practicing Your Swing With a Broom

Broom Drill No. 1: Check Your Posture

Photo 1: Stand erect, holding the broom horizontally in your fingers, across the top of your thighs.

Photo 2: By bending your knees, lower the broom a couple of inches. That produces the proper amount of knee-flex for the setup.

Photo 3: Now, pull the broom up with both hands until it sits at the crease formed by the top of your legs and your trunk. Tip your upper body forward over the broom, bending at the hips.

Remember the Learning Triangle: First check your posture from down the line in a full-length mirror. It should look similar to mine. Then close your eyes and concentrate on how it feels.

Broom Drill No. 2:
Check Your Spine Angle

Photo 1: Hold the broom vertically down the center of your back with your right hand behind your hips, your left hand above your head. Lean your head back so it touches the broom handle.

Photo 2: Get in your T-station and lean your spine forward. Maintaining your head against the broom keeps the spine straight. Look in a full-length mirror from down the line to check the amount of spine angle you have (it should be about 45 degrees from vertical).

Photo 3: Looking face-on in the mirror, check the amount of spine tilt to the right you have set at address (it should be about 15 degrees from vertical).

Again, remember the Learning Triangle: After you have checked your positions in the mirror, try getting in those same positions with your eyes closed. Then open your eyes and adjust accordingly. The posture and spine-angle drills will put your body in a good position from which to begin your swing.

1

2

3

1   2   3

Broom Drill No. 3:
For Pitch-and-Run Stroke,
Choke Down to Keep Left Wrist Flat

Photo 1: First, place wraps of tape at the handle-end of the broom to simulate the correct length for a driver, 5-iron and sand wedge.

Photo 2: Now, grip down to the tape that corresponds to the sand wedge and set up in a pitch-and-run position with a narrow, slightly open stance. Because you are choking down you will have a portion of the broom handle that is protruding above your hands. Put that against your left hip. You'll be using this address position later on for a pitch-and-run stroke.

Photos 3 and 4: Feel your pivot through the broom as you swing back and through. The broom handle helps promote keeping your left wrist flat and in line throughout the stroke.

The Golf Swing

4

Remember the Learning Triangle: Make the movement with your eyes closed to learn how your left wrist should feel through impact.

Broom Drill No. 4: Learn to Finish First

The most effective way to develop or check your full-swing balance is by starting at the finish.

Photo 1: In front of a full-length mirror, get in your setup position with the broom placed horizontally across the top of your spine, the broom bristles in your right hand and over your right shoulder.

Photo 2: Then turn to your finish position. To make sure your right shoulder is lower than your left, check to see that the bristles of the broom are lower than the handle.

Photo 3: Now simply reach around with your right hand and in its normal position put it on the broom. That is the correct finish position.

Remember the Learning Triangle: First, check your positions in the mirror against the photographs of me here, going from address to the finish. Then repeat the sequence with your eyes closed and concentrate on how this finish position feels. Do this several times a day until you can get into a proper finish position consistently.

1

2

3

1

Broom Drill No. 5:
Putting It All Together

Photo 1: Grip the broom with your left hand first, just below the marker tape for a driver's length, and continue through your normal grip and address routine (first putting the right hand on the broom, then finding the impact line with the broom bristles, which should be vertical, and finally finding your balance). The handle end of the broom should be just below your belt buckle (inset).

2   3   4

Photo 2: Now slowly go through all your swing positions, starting with the takeaway, turning your body along with the broom.

Photo 3: *To the top.* Look for the proper alignment of the back of your left hand and arm with the bristles of the broom. They should be square. Check this down the line in the full-length mirror.

Photo 4: *"Sit down."* On the downswing, move into a sitting position. Here the broom shaft should be about parallel to the floor and your target line, the bristles vertical to the floor.

Photo 5: *To impact.* The end of the broom should be in line with the side of your left hip, just like in Broom Drill No. 3. Check to be sure that your left wrist is flat, your right wrist is bent and the broom handle is leaning slightly forward (toward the target). Your hips at this stage should be from 30 to 40 degrees open to your target line. Your shoulders should be half as much open as your hips.

Photo 6: *To the finish.* Be sure the bristles of the broom are slightly lower than the handle, which indicates

6

5

your right shoulder is correctly lower than your left. Your weight should be predominantly on the outside of your left foot and toward the heel. Your left leg should be straight and your knees should be together.

Remember the Learning Triangle: First check each of these positions in the full-length mirror, then try each one with your eyes closed until you can feel them. Open your eyes and make the necessary adjustments.

Part II

The Golf Shot

When you are trying to make changes in your mechanics, your performance is likely to get worse. Look at what happened to my friend the doctor when I changed his putting routine. He went from an average of 36 putts a round (which is not very good) to more than 40 putts a round (which is disastrous) for the first six weeks or so. But suddenly, just when he was about to give up on his new routine, he started holing everything.

By the same token, if you are worried about performance—for instance, if you are concerned about the quality of the shots you are hitting—then your body will intu-itively resist making a change. When you are away from a practice range or a golf course and are not hitting shots, you can focus totally on learning the mechanics of the movements that you are making. You can focus on learn-ing to do the correct things with your body. *Now when you get on the practice tee and you actually start to hit shots, you should switch away from a mechanics or learning mode and into a performance mode.*

Why? Because this is like a dress rehearsal, like a scrimmage in other sports. There is no penalty for poor performance like there is in the actual game, but it is more performance oriented. This is where you are trying out the motions. And you are developing the sequence and timing of those motions. You are more oriented to the outcome than you were in your at-home practice.

4 | How to Practice

When you are practicing shots, you obviously need a ball, because the ball flight is your main source of performance feedback. And you need a target, something to relate your ball flight to. When you are practicing shots, *discipline yourself to always have a target and a picture in your mind of the shot you are about to hit*. Not only will that make your practice routines more interesting, but they will be more efficient and more productive as well.

For example, you should be visualizing a trajectory, a shot shape, where the ball is going to land and where it is going to finish. Let's say that on a scale of 1 to 4, a 4 represents a shot that is exactly like the one you visualized before you tried to hit it, including where the ball finishes. That's a perfect shot in relation to your plans.

A 3 would be a shot that isn't exactly like the one you pictured but is acceptable. Maybe it didn't go at exactly the right trajectory or maybe it had a little different shot shape than you pictured, but it ended up in a location that is OK. Maybe it would have been in the wrong side of the fairway or maybe just in the edge of the rough but in a decent lie. Or maybe it would have been on the green, but 40 feet from the hole instead of 10 feet. But if you hit this same shot on the course it wouldn't prevent you from carrying out the rest of your plan based on where it finished.

A 2 would be a shot that is not like the one you visualized and wouldn't be in an acceptable place. Maybe you caught it a little heavy and it is 20 yards short of your normal distance. Or maybe you pulled it or pushed it or hooked it or sliced it enough to miss the green and put it in a bunker. A 2 is unacceptable. It puts you in a position where you can't carry out your next stroke as you had planned.

Now a 1 would be a shot that is severely mis-hit. It would go into a water hazard, or out-of-bounds, or in a place where you might lose the ball, costing you a penalty stroke.

You need to be able to rate every shot you hit in practice on that scale of 1 to 4, which I am borrowing from my friend, Peter Sanders, founder and president of Golf Resource Associates. To do that, you must have a picture of each shot in your mind before you hit it, a habit you will certainly benefit from when we get to the issue of scoring on the course.

Earlier, we talked about blocked practice and random practice. In Part I on The Golf Swing, we used blocked practice almost exclusively. That is where you repeat the same mechanical motion over and over until it is imprinted into your motor memory system. In this section, we will use primarily random practice. That is where you change a variable on every shot. Maybe it's your target, or your ball flight, or your club. There is much research on effective learning that shows you will learn a specific skill faster if you do something else between tries.

The temptation on the practice range is to hit the same shot over and over, because you have the same club in your hand and you get into a rhythm. Say you are practicing with your driver. It's convenient to keep the same tee in the ground and just bend over to tee up another ball. It is easy to get into a pattern of just hitting the same shot repeatedly. But on the golf course you would never hit two drivers in a row (unless you are hitting a provisional ball). In fact, the only shot you might hit twice in a row is a putt, and then one would be a longer putt, the next a shorter one. A better practice alternative is to have, say, your sand wedge or pitching wedge or 5-iron readily available so between driver shots you can hit a pitch shot or a 5-iron to a completely different target. That will help to keep your mind sharp and is a much more realistic rehearsal for the golf course.

Before you begin a practice session, it's extremely helpful to have a plan that quickly outlines what you want to accomplish. Take two minutes and write it down on a

Before practicing, outline what you want to accomplish

card or piece of paper to remind you. Again, let's look at other sports. I have to believe that very few coaches walk out onto the practice field with their team in the afternoon and then start figuring out what they are going to do. They have already made a plan that they are about to implement. They know exactly what their team is going to practice for the next two hours or so. And so should you—if you want to make the most of your time on the range.

5 | Making Solid Contact

Before we start practicing actual shots on the range, learning to make solid contact between the club and ball is all important. The easiest way to learn to do this is by starting with the smallest shots (putts) and working up to the longest full-swing shots. I will give you one drill for each type of shot to help you learn to make solid contact. If you spend five minutes on each drill at the beginning of your practice sessions, you will be amazed at how much easier it will be to produce the shots you are working on.

Solid Contact, Putting:
Lay a Channel of Clubs

Making solid contact between putter and ball is essential to good putting. No matter how correct your alignment and stroke are, you must hit your putts consistently solid to hole an appreciable number. Here's how to perfect your contact. On the practice putting green, find a level putt of about 20 feet with no cup.

Photo 1: Place two clubs parallel to each other about six inches apart along that 20-foot putt and place a coin on the green within that channel of clubs. Now, using the same type of ball you normally play with, place it just in front of the coin, so the brand name letters are in line with your target and parallel to the channel of clubs.

Photo 2: With the same putting grip, setup and motion you learned in Part I, practice rolling the ball with your putter out the end of the channel.

Your two objectives: (1) The head of the putter should not touch the coin during the stroke, so the putter-

1

face contacts the ball slightly above the ball's equator; (2) the ball should roll so the lettering stays smoothly in line, not wobble. Keep practicing the motion you learned in Part I, until you begin to meet your objectives of solid contact and the lettering on the ball stays smoothly in line. Keep your eyes focused on the back of the ball until it is gone. Remind yourself to "watch for the grass under the ball" after you hit it.

The Channel Works for Hitting Solid Chips, Too

To learn how to make solid contact on your chips, use the same channel of clubs just off the practice putting green. Simply use the same chipping setup and stroke you learned in Part I (grip and ball position the same as for putting, but the handle of the club moved toward the target until the left wrist is flat; eyes no longer directly over the ball, so the sole of the club lies flat on the ground).

Again, using the same type of ball you normally play with and, say, an 8-iron, practice making short chipping strokes. The club should strike the ball, then the turf. It will do that if you remember to keep your right wrist bent and your left wrist flat through impact. Don't be concerned with where the ball ends up. Concentrate only on making solid contact.

Solid Contact on a Pitch-and-Run Stroke: Use a Bunker Rake as Your Guideline

1

Photo 1: On the practice tee, lay a bunker rake on the ground so the handle is pointed at your target. With a felt-tip pen, mark a few balls in quarters and color solid one of the quarters. Put a ball about a grip-length foward of the teeth-end of the rake and about two inches away from the shaft of the rake so the colored quarter faces your right toe (inside the target line).

Photo 2: From this ball position and using the full-swing grip pictured and discussed on pages 36-38, hit a few short pitch-and-runs with your sand or pitching wedge, concentrating on the basic technique you learned in Part I and focusing on the inside-back quarter of the ball. (Note: Except for putts, chips and bunker shots, always focus on the inside-rear quarter of the ball.) The bunker rake encourages you to keep the shaft of the club leaning forward (toward the target) through impact. Otherwise, your club will hit the teeth-end of the rake on the downswing. To do this, you must keep your right wrist bent and your left wrist flat through impact. The inside quarter of the ball encourages a downward and outward swinging of the club. Don't worry about where the ball goes. You should only be concerned with making solid contact, the club hitting the ball first, then the turf.

2

Use the Rake for Solid Contact
on Normal Pitch Shots, Too

Photo 1: Position your body with the same bunker rake you used for making solid contact on pitch-and-run shots, but move the ball farther forward (two grip-lengths from the teeth of the rake), so the club isn't swinging downward on as steep an angle. Again, use a quartered ball aligned at your right toe. Widen your stance a bit to allow for more lower-body thrust to accompany your pivot and arm swing, and assume the same setup and posture you learned in Part I for the full pitch shot.

Photo 2: Now, hit a few shots, concentrating on the clubhead swinging down into the ball on an angle similar to the one portrayed by the bunker rake—still from high to low but more level than for the pitch-and-run. Focus on the inside quarter of the ball. Repeat this drill until your clubhead contacts the ball, then the turf, making sure your hips turn through in support of your shoulders, arms and clubshaft.

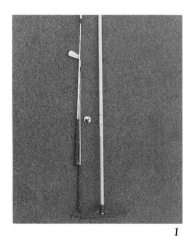

1   2

Bunker Rake Aids Solid Contact
for Pitching Cut Shot

On the practice ground, lay a long iron along your target line and place a bunker rake at a 20-degree angle across the club so the rake handle points left of your target (see photo). Assuming a slightly more open stance than for a normal pitch and positioning the ball an inch farther forward, practice hitting short shots with your sand wedge, making the clubhead swing back and through along the line of the bunker rake. For this stroke, you are purposely swinging from out to in. Concentrate on the reverse roll hinge with your hands and wrists, as demonstrated with the Ping-Pong paddles in Part I. This will result in a soft, high ball flight that falls slightly left to right.

Make clubhead swing back and through on line of rake

Paint a Line to Make Solid Contact on Irons and Fairway Woods

1

2

3

To make solid contact on full-swing shots when the ball is resting on the ground, you need to learn to make a divot in the right place.

Photo 1: A simple way to do this is to paint a line a few feet long on the grass on the practice tee. The line should be perpendicular to an imaginary target line. (Borrow a can of white spray paint from your course superintendent or club pro, the same kind of paint they use to mark ground under repair on the course.) Then set up to that line as if the ball were directly on it, opposite a point two inches inside your left heel, as you would if the ball were on the ground.

Photo 2: Make practice swings with your goal being to produce divots on the target side of the line. Ideally, the divot would start just at the front edge of that line and go toward the target. That way, you would be hitting the ball, then the turf, which is the key element to making solid contact when the ball is on the ground. Practice until you can consistently make your divots in the right place on the target side of the line.

Photo 3: Finally, set balls on the line and make swings with the same goal—to make the divots in the right place on the target side of the line. The ball is just in the way.

To Make Solid Contact with the Driver, Leave the Tee in the Ground

Most golfers who are poor drivers hit the ball too high on the clubface. Generally, their downswing planes are too steep. To encourage a shallower downswing plane and, therefore, contact lower on the face, make your goal to leave the tee in the ground after impact (see photo). To do this, concentrate on a more horizontal plane—feel as if you are swinging more around your body.

If you are topping the ball, the best advice I've heard is from the legendary teacher, Harvey Penick. Someone asked him once, "Harvey, I keep topping the ball. What do you think I ought to do?" Harvey said, "You need to swing lower."

If this advice fails, always remember to go back to the fundamentals outlined in Part I. First of all, review your ball position. When the ball is on the ground or teed down (for irons and fairway woods), it should be opposite a point two inches inside your left heel. For your driving club when the ball is teed up, it should be opposite your left heel. If you find that you are one of those rare individuals whose swing with the driver is too shallow, then tee the ball a little lower and try to break the tee off with your club on the through-swing.

6 | Direction

Every golf shot is made up of three dimensions: (1) direction, (2) distance and (3) trajectory. This chapter deals with direction, which you control with aim. So the focus of all the drills for direction will be related to proper alignment, and then a reflection of the ball's flight related to that alignment. No matter how good your swing or your ball striking is, if you are not good at aiming, you won't be effective. It is like shooting a gun. It doesn't matter how good your technique is—how smoothly you squeeze the trigger—if your sight is misaligned, you will never hit your target.

Use the Chalk Line Drill
to Perfect Putting Direction

At most hardware stores you can buy a carpenter's chalk line for about $3. A kit consists of a string and chalk.

Photo 1: Find a flat area on the practice putting green and snap a 10-foot chalk line back from the cup. (Don't worry about damaging the green. The chalk will dissolve under a light rain or sprinkler and will probably be gone by the next day.) Using the same setup and ball position you learned in Part I, practice six- to 10-foot putts along the chalk line. The putt can be slightly uphill, but should not have any sidehill break.

Photo 2: Aim the letters on the ball along the chalk line. You can use a striped range ball, but I prefer you practice putting with the same kind of ball you normally play with so you get accustomed to aiming the letters and looking at them while you make your stroke.

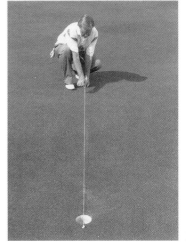

1

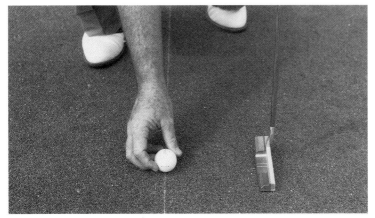

2

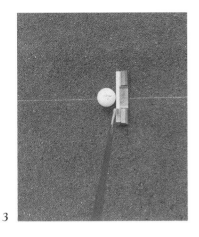

3

4

Photo 3: Set the putterblade behind the ball so it is perpendicular to the letters, while assuming your grip and stance as outlined in Chapter 1.

Photo 4: Using the same putting stroke you learned in Chapter 1—the motion coming from the shoulders— strike the ball so the letters roll directly down the chalk line.

The Club-channel Drill
Promotes Accurate Chipping Direction

The same drill you used for learning to make solid contact in chipping is also effective for improving your direction.

Photo 1: Place two clubs on the fringe parallel to each other about six inches apart and aligned at a target on the practice green. Using your address routine, align the face of your chipping club—anything from a 5-iron up to a sand wedge—and assume the chipping address position you learned in Chapter 1. Remember, the chipping address is identical to the putting address but with the clubshaft leaning forward until your left wrist is flat and your right wrist is bent.

Photo 2: Now practice chipping balls out of the channel, using the pivot motion you learned in Chapter 1. Concentrate only on the direction the ball starts on and rolls.

Remember: When practicing shots on the range, discipline yourself to always have a target and picture in your mind. Visualize a trajectory, a shot shape, where the ball is going to land and where it will finish.

1

2

For Pitching, the Bunker Rake Promotes Pinpoint Direction, Too

To help you learn proper direction for your pitch shots, use the same bunker rake, but this time focus on the handle end of the rake.

As in the photograph at left, on the practice tee, place the rake on the ground, aligned at a target. That represents your target line. Now, place a ball two inches from the rake on your side of the handle and use your address routine to assume the normal address position you learned for a pitch shot. (To review from Chapter 1, grip the club with your left hand first, then your right hand, align the clubface at your target—perpendicular to the rake handle—then align your feet slightly open to the rake handle.) Before you hit the ball, visualize its starting direction along the path of the rake, and "see" in your mind's eye the ball's flight along that same path, then make your pitching motion and let the motion hit the ball.

For Full-swing Direction, Use an Intermediate Target

Photo 1: On the practice range, first find a target to hit balls to—maybe it's a distant tree or part of a building or fence. Then stick a clubshaft or an umbrella into the ground about six to 10 feet in front of the ball and in line with your target. Put the shaft on an angle, leaning away from you.

Photo 2: Practice hitting shots so the ball starts directly over that shaft. If you are practicing a draw, the shaft

1

2

should be placed on a line to the right of your distant target; it should be on a line to the left of your distant target for a fade. Your goal is to have the ball start right over that shaft.

Photo 3: As you hit practice shots, also rehearse the way your eyes should track at address from the ball to the shaft to the distant target, back to the shaft and back to the inside-rear quarter of the ball. To do this, your head should rotate with your right eye coming under to look at the shaft and the target, so you don't come out of your address posture.

3

7 | Trajectory

Trajectory control is important from a number of different perspectives. Let's take chipping, for example. It is very difficult to plan a chip if you don't have the ability to control the trajectory on which the ball travels. If you can't control trajectory, you can't predict how far the ball will roll after landing. The same is true for pitching. If the greens are firm and fast, you may need to use a higher trajectory shot to get the ball to stop rolling near the pin. If you're pitching up a two-tiered green with the pin on the second tier, you may need to use a lower trajectory to get the ball to roll up the hill to the hole.

In the full swing, controlling the trajectory of the shot is especially important when playing in the wind or to elevated greens or under or over a tree limb.

Trajectory Starts on the Putting Green

In putting, of course, trajectory is always on the ground. But the ground is not always level. Putts have a tendency to have a shape to them, curving to the left or to the right. Green-reading really boils down to the management of the relationship between the momentum you give the ball and the force of gravity. Let me illustrate. If you were standing a few feet away from me and I tossed you a ball and I didn't throw it hard enough, gravity would pull it down to the ground before it got to you. So I would have to give it enough momentum to get it to you before gravity started to pull it down. In tossing that ball, I am trying to decide where I want gravity to overcome momentum. The same thing is true in shooting a basketball. You toss the ball to the top of its arc and let gravity carry it into the basket.

Likewise, when you look across a green, what you are really trying to decide is where you want gravity to overcome momentum. Because the instant gravity starts to overtake the momentum you gave the ball, the ball will start to move down the slope.

1

2

Putt Through the Gate
to Feel Trajectory

    You can make a small gate from a clothes hanger, similar to the metal gates used in croquet, or use a pair of tees, positioned a few inches apart.

    Photo 1: First find a sloping 20-foot putt on the practice green and try to read its break. Determine where you want gravity to overtake momentum. At that point, place the gate in the green.

    Photo 2: Next, aim the letters on the ball at the gate. Try to roll the ball with enough momentum to get through the gate, and let gravity take the ball from the gate to the hole. Keep practicing with your gate until you get the hang of seeing where you should aim your breaking putts and how hard you need to roll them. Remember that the gate can be adjusted up or down the slope and closer to or farther from the hole.

Put a Shaft in the Ground to Simulate Trajectory in Chipping

Remember the clubshaft you used for the full-swing intermediate target drill? Now you can put it to good use here as well to learn the proper trajectory in chipping.

Photo 1: On a normal chip shot on the practice green, say a 20-footer, first toss a few balls underhand to get a feel for the roll. Take note of what angle the ball needs to descend on and where it needs to land. Now

pick the club you think will produce that angle (this may take some experimentation).

Photo 2: Then hit a few chips using the method outlined in Part I. (To review: Using a putting grip, the lower body remains stable, the motion coming primarily from the arms and shoulders, like in putting.) Again, notice what angle the ball needs to descend on and where it needs to land.

3

4

Photo 3: Next place the shaft in the green at the point and on the angle necessary for the ball to land and roll the correct distance to the hole.

Photo 4: Then simply try to chip balls down that shaft. Visualize a trajectory and landing spot. Depending on the club you use (a sand wedge to a 5-iron) and on the length of shot, you can change the angle of the shaft in the green. A higher shot with a more lofted club, for instance, requires a more vertical shaft in the green; a lower shot with a less lofted club requires a more horizontal shaft.

Ladder Drill Promotes
Pitching Trajectories

This drill requires a six-foot stepladder and is a quick way to learn to hit normal pitches on different trajectories. Place the ladder about 10 yards in front of you. With your pitching wedge or your sand wedge, try to pitch the ball between the different rungs of the ladder. Use your normal pitching technique as outlined in Part I—ball positioned two inches inside your left heel, stance 20 degrees open to the target line. Narrow your stance to lower the trajectory; widen it to raise the trajectory.

Remember: When practicing shots on the range, discipline yourself to always have a target and picture in your mind. Visualize a trajectory, a shot shape, where the ball is going to land and where it will finish.

Practice with a Tree
to Learn Full-swing Trajectories

To master the different trajectories for full shots, you need to have a reference point. It could be clouds in the sky, or a distant treeline. But you must have something to shoot over and under and around. In my opinion, trajectory also includes curving the ball while hitting it different heights.

1

Photo 1: To hit the ball lower on a full shot, make a pitch-and-run or knockdown type of swing with a narrower than normal stance (inset). The ball position should not change—it should still be two inches inside the left heel. Some people advocate playing the ball back in the stance, but I disagree. That only causes you to start the ball more to the right. Put your hands forward until

2

your left wrist is flat at address. Simply let your pitch-and-run shot grow up into a knockdown shot.

Photo 2: To hit the ball higher, widen your stance more than for a normal shot, and put the shaft back in its normal position (inset). The ball position is just inside your left heel. *This technique requires a good lie,* because you probably are going to hit the ball on the upswing.

3

Photo 3: To curve the ball from right to left, aim your body lines parallel to the line you want the ball to start on and aim the clubface where you want the ball to finish. You might play the ball a ball-width farther back in your stance. Then swing along your body lines (inset).

4

Photo 4: To curve the ball from left to right, the same principle applies. Again aim your body lines parallel to the line you want the ball to start on and aim the club-face where you want the ball to finish. You might play the ball a ball-width farther forward in your stance. Then swing along your body lines (inset).

8 | Distance

Just as it is essentially the job of aim to control direction and it is mostly the job of clubface loft to control trajectory, it is primarily the job of your motion to control distance. The key to distance control is to be completely at ease with everything other than distance when you putt, chip, pitch or hit a full shot. Most people who don't have good distance control are still concerned about something else when they hit the shot.

Sometimes you hear that you should take extra club to allow for a mis-hit on approach shots. I disagree. Always anticipate solid contact. That is the only way you will ever become consistent in controlling your distance. The key is to learn to make solid contact almost every time you hit a shot before you try to do anything else.

The only device you have to measure distance with is your eyes. Give them enough time to do their job. Studies have shown that rapid eye movement in sports like golf is almost always damaging. So move your eyes very slowly back and forth between the ball and your target. Moving your eyes along the ground from the target to the ball has the same effect as a measuring wheel. If your eyes are jumping back and forth from the target to the ball, they never have a chance to focus at either length, so there is some level of confusion. Just move your eyes slowly.

The Ribbon Drill Promotes Distance Control in Putting and Chipping

To fine-tune your distance control on the putting green, you need a line that is specific for distance and general for direction. Create such a line by placing a piece of ribbon several feet long on the practice green. Stick a tee in each end so it stays in place. Putt or chip to that ribbon from various distances, trying to make the ball finish within a foot or two of the ribbon (see photo). Don't worry at all about direction. You want to simply develop your feel for distance. Remember to let your eyes track slowly from the ball to the ribbon back to the ball, and try to visualize the ball rolling along the ground.

Note: This drill can be done indoors on carpet if the speed is similar to a real golf course green. You can use tape instead of ribbon for your target.

Use the Stairstep Drill
to Further Enhance Distance Feel

Again on the practice green, a great way to develop feel for longer distances is to place several clubs on the green in a stairstep pattern (see photo). Then hit six to 10 putts up and down the "stairs," each time stroking the ball so it rolls one club-length farther or shorter than the last effort. Concentrate on making the ball roll exactly the correct distance with only minimal regard for direction. Soon you will learn to focus solely on the distance you need to hit the ball, exclusive of concern for direction, trajectory or solid contact.

The Towel Drill Enhances
Distance Feel on Pitches

An enjoyable way to learn to fly your pitches the right distance is to do what Tom Kite does. He lays several towels on the practice ground in five-yard increments, starting at about 25 or 30 yards and going out as far as he wants. The trick is, he doesn't shoot at the same towel twice in a row. Change towels every time you hit a shot. The object is to land the ball on the towel, because you are trying to visualize and control the distance the ball travels in the air.

"Call Your Shot" to Practice
Full-swing Distance Control

Your priority with every club you are using, even with your driver, is to have a specific distance you want to hit the ball in the air before you swing. On the range, pick a spot and visualize landing the ball on that spot. Key on which club you need to select and how hard you need to swing to make the ball go the distance you want.

This is random practice. Change clubs between shots. Maybe you hit a driver, then a 9-iron, then a 5-iron, then another driver. Each time, simulate the playing conditions of a golf course. It creates little benefit to simply hit 30 drivers in a row to an undefined target. That might get you into a nice rhythm and you might start hitting the ball fairly well, but you are only kidding yourself. It will be difficult to make the transition to the golf course. You will improve your on-course ball striking much more quickly if your practice sessions are shorter and more specific.

9 | In the Bunker

In the drills for making solid contact at the beginning of this section, we discussed three types of pitch shots: a normal pitch, a pitch-and-run and cut shot. In the bunker, there are likewise three basic types of shots: a standard bunker shot, a buried lie shot and a short shot from a good lie.

In the bunker you are not trying to hit the ball. You are trying to hit the sand. And you do that by adjusting the ball position. For a standard bunker shot, you play the ball slightly forward of your ball position for a normal pitch and then make your normal pitching swing.

With your sand wedge, you must move some sand along with the ball. The club enters the sand behind the ball and throws it out of the bunker on a cushion of sand. The weight of the sand you must move is about the equivalent of three golf balls. So you have the weight of four balls to move out of the bunker. Obviously, this requires a bigger swing, like hitting a driver with the head cover left

Photo 1: For a normal bunker shot, adjust your ball position slightly more forward than for a standard pitch (inset).

1

2

Photo 2: A swing that would be required for a 30-yard pitch (inset) would result in a 10-yard bunker shot.

on. I usually count on a 3-to-1 ratio. A swing that would hit a standard pitch 30 yards would hit a bunker shot 10 yards. A stroke that would send a standard pitch 60 yards would result in a 20-yard bunker shot.

For a Buried Lie,
Use Your Pitch-and-run Stroke

When the ball is buried in the sand, don't panic. Just pretend you are hitting a pitch-and-run.

Photo 1: Play the ball slightly forward of the pitch-and-run ball position, however, so the club enters the sand behind the ball.

Photo 2: Because the clubhead will be moving on more of a descending angle through impact; the follow-through will be minimal. The ball will come out lower with more roll than on a normal bunker shot, so allow for it.

1

2

1

For a Shorter Bunker Shot
Use Cut-shot Pitching Motion

For a short, high shot, you want to replicate a cut shot. The cut-shot swing is from out to in (Photo 1), using a reverse roll of the left hand and wrist through impact (Photo 2). Again, you want the club to enter the sand behind the ball, which will come out soft and with more backspin than a normal sand shot.

2

Part III

The Golf Score

In many other sports—football, basketball, soccer, to name three—the objective is to take the ball and move it to the other end of the playing field and put it in the goal. Golf should be no different.

You start at the tee, which is your end of the field, the part of the playing area where you need to be somewhat conservative because mistakes are very costly. An especially poor shot with your driving club is much more likely to put you in a bad situation than a mis-hit shot with a shorter club. You don't want to get overly defensive on the tee, but you do want to be cautious and realistic.

Once you have put your tee shot in play, you move the ball along to the best degree you can with advancement and approach shots until you get into the scoring zone, where you try to put the ball into the goal.

That is why this section of the book is divided into three chapters, working from the green back to the tee: (1) The Scoring Zone, (2) Advancement and Approach Shots, and (3) The Tee Shot.

We will start with the scoring zone, because unless you are proficient in that area, the rest of it doesn't matter. It is like a football team that plays tremendously well until it gets inside the 20-yard line and then can't score any points. Racking up all that yardage is meaningless.

Filling Your Toolbox

Before you can begin, however, you need to have a clear understanding of your strengths and weaknesses. The essence of getting to know your game is making a realistic assessment of what strokes and what clubs you can consistently control the ball with. That's because what you are looking for is predictability, a high degree of certainty related to what the ball is going to do when you hit it, or chip it or putt it. You can't make a strategic plan on the course based on the execution of shots you can do successfully only on occasion.

What you need to do in the practice area, therefore, is determine what degree of certainty you have with each of your clubs and with the different types of shots, whether they be fades, draws, high shots or low shots, pitches, chips or bunker shots. You are, in effect, filling up your toolbox. So when you get on the course and you are confronted with a specific situation, you can reach in that toolbox and find the right tool for the job. Obviously, a tour player has more tools in his box than, say, a 10-handicapper, and they are probably higher-precision tools. So on the course tour players have more options and can play more types of shots. They seldom if ever try a shot with the wrong tool. And they learn about their tools through practice. The key is knowing what you've got in your toolbox and not trying to play out of a tour player's toolbox, unless you are one.

Ball hitting during this assessment process needs to be random rather than blocked. You need to "play" a round of golf or two on the practice range. For example, imagine the fairway shape and width and hit a tee shot. Then with whatever target you have on your practice range, imagine an approach shot and hit it. Take the scorecard of your home course to the practice tee and simulate your golf course there.

Remember the 1-to-4 rating scale introduced in Part II? If the majority of the shots you are hitting, say with your driver, are coming up 1s and 2s, then you are driving with the wrong club. If you come away from this assessment having hit half of your shots in an unacceptable way with a particular club, that's a club you should not yet be trying to use on the golf course, where the emphasis is on shooting the best score you can. Each person has his or her own risk-management system in terms of acceptability. I don't like to attempt shots on the course that I don't feel good about being able to hit eight out of 10 times. And I don't want the other two to be too bad. So I am going to hit shots and use clubs that I feel certain about 80 percent of the time. I'll leave the rest of my tools in my toolbox and continue to work on them off the course. *The biggest mistake people make is going on the golf course and trying to hit shots they can only hit on rare occasions.*

By far the most important ingredient to playing and scoring well is keeping the ball under control. Sure, I could drive Davie Allison's racecar, but if I tried to go as fast as he does, I most certainly would have an accident because I don't have the ability to control it at that speed. Controlling your golf ball on the course is directly dependent on your ability to honestly assess your capabilities, and a lot of people have difficulty doing that.

Play the First Hole
Like You're Making the Turn

In warming up, the overall goal is to get your mind and your body ready to play the game. Think again of other sports. When a football team comes onto the field to warm up before the game, what are the players doing? They are stretching, loosening up, trying to stay relaxed, getting familiar with the surroundings and conditions. They are not trying to acquire any skills. They are getting their bodies and minds prepared to use the skills that they already have. For golfers, stretching in the locker room or any type of exercise that would get the body warmed up is more effective for that purpose than hitting golf balls because they are less likely to become overly focused on swing mechanics. Now you go to the practice tee and hit balls for two reasons: (1) To get a feel for the timing and the rhythm of the motion, and (2) to eliminate the anxious, uneasy or awkward feeling most golfers have on the first tee. Ideally, you want to feel like you are making the turn when you go to the first tee. That means doing some random practice where you "play" a few holes on the range. Hit a tee shot, then a 7-iron, then a chip. Hit a tee shot, a fairway wood and a pitch. For each shot go through your routine. Make it feel like you have already started playing and making the shots count.

Warming up on the putting green, you should have two objectives: (1) Getting a feel for the speed of the greens and (2) becoming comfortable with your putting routine. To develop feel for speed, hit several balls across the green in different directions concentrating on how far the ball is rolling. For shorter putts, use only one ball and go through your normal procedure each time. Read the green, for example. Don't stand there and hit casual putts. Get serious about each one, just like you are going to do on the course.

Hit some three-footers, because you will get a few of those, but don't putt, say, three in a row from the same place. Instead, place them in a circle around the hole so each one is different. Again, go through your normal routine for each putt. On longer putts, don't just putt the ball up by the hole and then knock it away. Roll it up to the hole and then roll it in. Again, the objective is to be already into the round when you go to the first tee.

10 The Scoring Zone

Most golfers in the scoring zone (around the green and on the green) are not focused to the degree that they need to be. I would prefer with few exceptions for you to be trying to hole the ball out with every shot within 50 yards of the flag. Sometimes, because of the severity of the situation, you might have to adjust your plan and play a safer shot, but most of the time on a pitch or a chip or even a bunker shot I would like your objective to be to put the ball in the hole, not to get it close.

One general rule of thumb when you are in the scoring zone: Unless you have to play over an object (a bunker, water or a tree), usually the lowest trajectory shot that will work is the best shot to play. The shot that stays closest to the ground is the highest-percentage option for most players. For example, the shot that you are least likely to mis-hit is a putt. So as you move back off the green, all you are trying to do is get the ball on the green and let the shot turn into a putt. Read the break based on the same principles of green-reading we discussed earlier.

Before you play any shot around the green, you need to choose three things: (1) Where you want the ball to land, (2) how far it needs to roll after it lands and (3) the trajectory you want it to land on. Then, based on your past experience in practice and play, pick the swing and club that will meet those three objectives. It's easy to overanalyze a shot on the course. Don't. Try to let your instincts and your body take over so you can feel the shot you need to play. Remember, you're not learning, you're performing.

Putting on the Course

On the green during a round, you need to use the same putting skills you learned in practice. You still need to visualize the point where you want gravity to overcome momentum. On the practice green you learned to use a gate. Now, mentally transfer that image to the green on the course. When you are reading a putt, you should be looking for the spot where the gate would go.

For many people, mental imagery can really work. An example is my doctor friend's son, who was one of the

placekickers for the University of Alabama. He was always an excellent kicker in practice, but his first two college seasons he struggled in games. Then the summer after his sophomore year he practiced kicking through a goalpost that had a utility pole behind it. The utility pole had a transformer on it at the trajectory that a good kick would be on. He learned to kick the ball directly at that transformer. During his junior year, he used that image of the transformer every time he tried a field goal or extra point. If he had a right-to-left wind, in his mind he shifted the transformer to the right a bit, and vice versa. When he went onto the field in a game, what he saw was that transformer (see illustration). He didn't see the crowd, he didn't hear the noise. The result is that during his last two seasons he rarely if ever missed on kicks of reasonable distance. This image worked because it took his mind off the mechanics of kicking. The same principles will work in putting on the course, or any shot for that matter.

Study Chip Shots from the Hole Back

When the ball is off the green, you are trying to get it on the green and let it turn into a putt. So you should read the roll part of the shot first (A). That tells you where you want the ball to land and how far you want it to run. How far you want it to run tells you the trajectory you need to use (B). The trajectory coupled with your lie tell you what club and which of your shots to use (C).

Imagine a Shaft in the Ground
to Determine Correct Trajectory

When the ball is farther from the green, say 25 to 75 yards, you need to use one of three types of pitches. To play a standard pitch shot, the majority of the time you should use your sand wedge. Occasionally you might hit a standard pitch with your pitching wedge. For a cut shot always use your sand wedge because the only reason to use that type of stroke is for maximum trajectory. A pitch-and-run you can play with any club from a 5- or 6-iron to your sand wedge, depending on how much you want the ball to run after it lands.

Shot selection often depends on what you are best at. Some players are more comfortable hitting a standard pitch, others would lean toward the pitch-and-run. Whichever shot you choose to play, first select a landing point and landing trajectory. Remember the angled shaft in the ground in Chapter 7? Imagine that same shaft on the course. Ask yourself where on the green (or short of the green) do you want that imaginary shaft, and on what angle do you want it. After you have acquired your mental image, play whatever stroke with whatever club your instincts and experience tell you to use. Don't try to analyze it. Don't try to go through some checklist. Just visualize that shaft and if your instincts say, for example, "pitch-and-run with a pitching wedge," take out the club, go through your routine and let your body make the swing that will produce that shot.

Before Hitting Bunker Shots, Predict the Trajectory First

When you are playing a shot from sand, first anticipate the trajectory and then let that dictate the landing point of your ball. Photo 1: For example, if you have a buried lie, the technique outlined in Chapter 9 will send the ball out fairly low and running. Photo 2: You shouldn't try to do anything about that. Just plan for it.

If you have a closely cut pin (near your side of the green), the ball will probably run past the hole. You should accept that fact and assume that you will probably need three shots to get the ball into the hole instead of two. In the sand, and elsewhere, always look for the easiest shot to play. You will save many strokes throughout the rest of your golfing life.

1

2

11 Advancement and Approach Shots

Golf is primarily a game of strategy. In any game of strategy—shooting billiards or playing chess, for example—you have to have the ability to plan at least two or three moves ahead. The same skill is necessary in golf. When you get on the tee, you should have a plan for the entire hole, even though you may not execute it perfectly every time. Unfortunately, many players go to the tee and hit the ball and then go find it and start trying to figure out what to do from there.

Build your strategy from the green back. Look at the green and decide what angle you would prefer to shoot into it from, then figure out how to get the ball within reach of the green and on that angle for your approach. On par 4s and 5s, in your mind you will have created a straight or zigzag line from the tee to the green. Your tee and advancement shots need to keep the ball near that line, until you get into the scoring zone. When you reach a point where it is reasonable to expect to hit the ball on the green, then you are hitting an approach shot.

Think One Shot Ahead

Sometimes there are greens and pin placements where you would like a little longer shot so you can hit the ball high enough to stop it. It is difficult to hit a high, short shot. It is a matter of staying at least one shot ahead of yourself in your planning. I had a student once—a very good player—who was leading a tournament in our city. He telephoned me and said, "I need to come and see you. I'm hitting the ball really well, but I'm not hitting my part wedges well at all." So we did some work early the next morning before his final round and he started hitting his part wedges a little better. After the lesson was over and he was walking away, he said, "Boy, I am really glad we worked on this, because there are three holes on the back nine of the course we are playing where if I hit my really good tee shot, I have a part wedge left." I said, "Why would you want to hit your best tee shot and leave yourself your weakest shot, the shot you are most concerned about? Maybe on those holes you should drive with a 4-

wood and leave yourself a full 9-iron to the green." Sometimes the solution to a problem is so obvious that we fail to notice it.

On Approach Shots,
Pretend There's No Flag

The key to executing successful approach shots is making a realistic blend of the target areas that are available and your *current* skills. One of the techniques I have found helpful is to look at the green as if you didn't know where the flag was and then decide what part of the green you would shoot for if you were just trying to hit the green. Most of the time that's where you ought to shoot, regardless of where the flag is.

The more you begin to shoot into the corners of the greens, the more damaging your mistakes are, for two reasons. (1) You are more likely to miss the green, and (2) if you miss the green on the same side as the pin, you usually have a difficult up-and-down because you have no green to work with. Corner pin placements create double jeopardy.

I played in the 1969 U.S. Open, at Champions in Houston. After the first round I saw my friend, the late Joe Dey, then Executive Director of the United States Golf Association, in the clubhouse. I made a laughing comment that the pins sure were difficult. He looked up from his lunch, smiled at me and said, "Well, they are only hard if you shoot at them."

Then he went on to explain that in every round of the U.S. Open, the committee would set six fairly generous pins, easy to get to; six that were reasonably difficult to get to, and six that only an idiot would shoot at. He said it was important in the U.S. Open for a player to be able to recognize which of those three types of pin placements he was facing on each hole of the round and to know which ones to shoot at. It was a great lesson for me because I was making the pins hard—I was shooting at all of them.

Pick Your Spots

Playing approach shots is like other sports. There are times when you are on offense and times when you are on defense; there are times when you have the ball and times when the other team has the ball. When the pin location is difficult, the other team has the ball. That is not the time to get aggressive and try to attack. You have to look for your openings, you have to pick your spots, and be aggressive when the opportunity presents itself.

Hit to Specific Targets on Advancement Shots

The most common mistake I see made in advancement shots is having too general a target. You need to be as precise with your target selection, your routine and your execution as you would be for a shot into the green. In fact, one of the mental techniques I give to my students is to have them imagine an actual green, complete with a flagstick, in the landing area of their advancement

shot (see photo). This image doesn't have to be a green. It could be a yardage sign you remember from your practice area. You may have a target area for, say, your second shot on a par 5, that is 60 yards wide. Know that you have a large margin of error so you stay relaxed on the shot, but visualize and aim for a specific point within that 60 yards.

Lay Up Intelligently

Laying up intelligently means eliminating as many problems as you can with club selection. As an example, let's say you have a shot that is 200 yards from the green, which is fronted by a pond (see diagram). You decide it's unrealistic to go for the green, so you plan to lay up. Say the pond is 20 yards across, so you have 180 yards to the pond. There is no point in trying to hit the ball 178 yards, because (1) you are liable to catch a hard spot in the fairway and run into the lake or (2) such a close lay up, even if executed perfectly, will leave you with a delicate partial pitch over the water. Instead, plan to play a 100- to 125-yard shot (3), which will leave you well short of the water, so you can make a full swing on your next shot from, say, 75 to 100 yards, with one of your wedges or short irons.

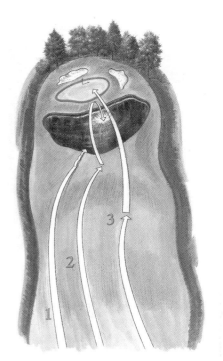

On Lay Ups, Look for the Best Angle

Laying up doesn't just mean leaving it short. It also means positioning for the next shot. A lot of golfers always hit a lay-up shot straight at the flag (A). That might not be the right line. Think about the angle on which you want to shoot at the flag on your next shot. It might be preferable to get the ball over to the side of the fairway, giving you a better angle into the green, so you don't have to come over a bunker, for example (B).

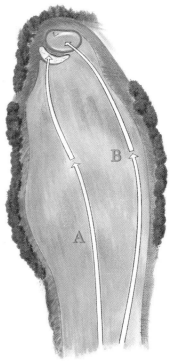

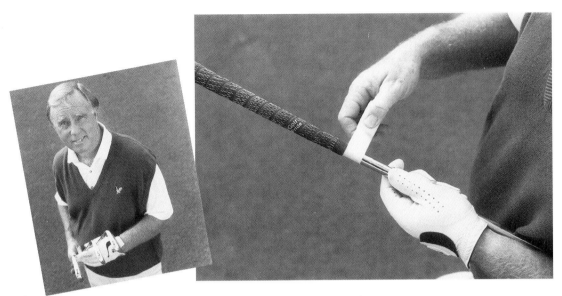

On Approach Shots, Use Your Red, Yellow and Green Clubs

I was teaching at a golf school a couple of years ago and was helping students chart their performance with the different clubs. Based on the outcome of this testing, I put different colored bands of tape on each club (see photos). A green club was one they could hit with enough accuracy to shoot at any pin they wanted to. Referring to the six-six-six pin settings used in the U.S. Open, which I discussed earlier, these clubs could shoot at all those pins. For the average player, that might be only the wedges or maybe the 9-iron. I put yellow tape on the group of clubs they could hit reasonably well. These might be the 8-iron through the 5-iron. The yellow clubs could shoot at the middle six settings and the easy six, but not the most difficult six. Then there were the clubs with red bands of tape. These might be long irons and woods. If the students were to aim at the green with these clubs, they needed to aim at only the biggest part of it and away from any trouble, such as bunkers or water.

You can put similar tape on your clubs, as well. It will help you discipline yourself on the course when you pull a club out of the bag. It's just like a traffic light: Green means go for it; yellow means caution—be careful; and red means danger, stop. Whether you put the tape on your clubs or not, remember that with some of your clubs you have a green light, some a yellow light and some a red light.

On Advancement and Approach Shots Focus Positively on a Target

One of the keys to shooting low scores is under-standing the difference between strategy and execution. For every advancement and approach shot, (1) first look at all the potential risks until you have your plan—your strat-egy—formed. Then (2) execute your plan positively.

In other words, *deal with where you don't want the ball to go in your strategy, not in your stroke*. Otherwise, that would be like driving your car down the street trying to miss the buildings. You don't do that. You know where the car goes—on the road, in your lane—so that is where your mind and your eyes are focused. You observe the other things around you, but your objective is to drive in that lane. It is not to miss the cars that are parked on the sides of the streets. The way to be sure of not doing the wrong thing is by focusing on doing the right thing, not by trying to avoid doing the wrong thing.

12 | The Tee Shot

You should have already developed your plan for the entire hole before you hit the tee shot. You should know exactly where you want to put the ball on every shot all the way to the ideal location on the green. The only objective of the tee shot, then, is to place the ball in position for your next shot, be it an advancement shot or an approach shot, or a putt on a par 3. Remember, we are on our end of the playing field, so mistakes here are costly. Now is the time to be a bit cautious with strategy.

Your Second Serve

Five-time British Open champion Peter Thomson once likened the tee shot to the second serve in tennis. The objective is to get it in so you can keep playing. Sure, it's fun to powder the ball as far as you can, but if you're serious about shooting the lowest score possible, you should keep that gorilla strategy for the driving range.

On the course, once you have picked the location in the fairway you want to shoot at, pick the appropriate club and try to be precise with your directional target. Use the same image you might use for an advancement shot, whether it be a flagstick or a yardage marker or whatever. Be specific with your distance parameter as well. Don't just try to hit the ball as far as you can hit it. Try to make it go the right distance, whatever that comfortable distance is for you.

Be realistic with your club selection for tee shots. I see a lot of golfers who are hung up on playing the "right" shot. "If I don't hit a driver from the tee," they say to themselves, "the guys I'm playing with will think there is something wrong with me, that I'm not a good player." Well, all that hitting the driver without the ability to do so consistently does for these golfers is *prove* they are not very good players in terms of scoring. Unless you are laying up, your No. 1 goal from the tee should be to hit the longest club you *know* you can hit in the fairway. It doesn't make any difference if it is a 6-iron or a 3-iron or a 3-wood or a driver. It takes much more courage to make a conservative decision than to make an aggressive decision. You don't have to feel ashamed if you are playing to your strengths or away from your weaknesses, because all great players do that. Instead, you should pat yourself on the back for having the discipline to do so.

On the Tee Shot, Pick a Precise Target

Once you have picked the general location in the fairway you want to shoot at, pick a club for that distance. Then, within the context of that bigger area, be precise about where you try to make the ball go. Use your image of a flagstick or yardage sign, and shoot for that spot. Don't just try to hit the ball as far as possible. Try to make it go a specific distance to a specific target.

Which Side of the Tee Should You Hit From?

Where you tee the ball is dictated by two factors: the characteristics of the hole and your shot tendencies. Generally, you want to hit from a position so the angle of your tee shot is going away from the most severe trouble. Say you are playing a hole with water on the right side. Illustration 1: The more you tee your ball on the right side of the tee, the better an angle back into the middle of the fairway you would have. Conversely, if the trouble is on the left, teeing up on the left gives you an angle away from that trouble.

Illustration 2: Given a straightaway hole with a problem on each side, someone who draws the ball should tee up on the left side of the tee. Because that person can then use the entire width of the fairway for the shape of

Illustration 1   *Illustration 2*

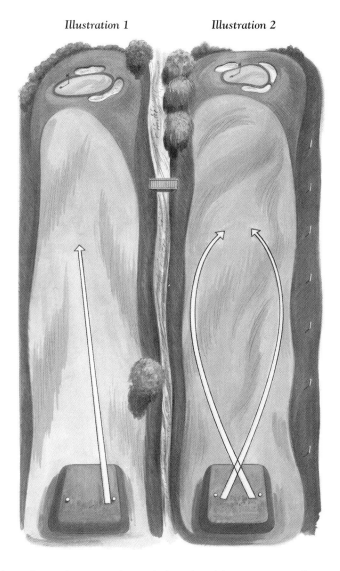

that shot. Conversely, a fader should tee up on the right side of the tee. Think of a placekicker in football. Right-footed kickers would prefer to kick from the left hash mark because their kicks tend to curve from right to left. Left-footed kickers would prefer to kick from the right hash mark. It gives them a better angle.

Playing Irons from the Tee

Right: When playing an iron from a tee, usually on a par 3, most golfers tee the ball too high. Left: You should tee the ball down by pushing the tee into the ground until the ball looks like it is sitting up on the very top of the grass. You want to replicate the same lie you would have in the fairway, but make it a good lie. And always tee it. Your chance of making solid ball-club contact is just that much better.

On Par 3s, Give Yourself the Best Possible Angle

The tee shot on a par 3 is the one place on the course where you are in total control of your options. Within limits, of course, you alone can decide where you want to shoot from. When you're standing on the tee of a par-3 hole, first notice where the pin is. Try to take the bunkers or water out of play as much as possible before you hit. Illustration: Is the pin behind a bunker on the left? If so, playing from the right side of the tee gives you your best angle to the hole. The reverse is true when the pin is behind a bunker on the right.

On Recovery Shots, Don't Be Columbus

Even the best of golfers can't always adhere to their preconceived strategy for a hole. Everyone hits a wayward shot now and again. You may be moving the ball along your basic strategy line and suddenly find yourself in the trees because of a misplayed shot. What then? You have put yourself in a situation where you need to make a recovery.

It is like being on a trip in your car and making a wrong turn. Now you have two options: (1) You can stop and get directions or check the map to get back on the original road with the least amount of negative effect on your trip. Or (2) you can start wandering around cross-country, trying to find your own way. You can go exploring, like Columbus.

It's amazing how many people in their cars refuse to stop and ask directions or check the map. They are too stubborn to admit they made a mistake and they only make matters worse. The same is true in golf. Almost always it is better to get back on your original plan immediately, to minimize the risk. You should make sure an errant shot doesn't cost you more than one stroke, and it might not cost you any strokes if you hit an approach close to the pin and hole the putt. Your original plan was sound and it still is.

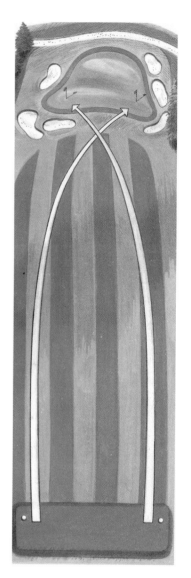

Almost Always, Pitch Out Safely

Here I am in the woods after my drive on a par 5. Now I have two options: (1) I can go exploring and try to hit a career shot through a small opening (X) and maybe get the ball on an adjacent fairway. Then, I would have to figure out how to hit my next shot on or somewhere near the green. If I'm lucky I might have a chance of making a par. But I've also introduced the opportunity to lose two or three shots on the hole, rather than just one. (2) I can pitch back to my original strategy line (0). If I do that, I have used one stroke to get back into the game. Unless I hit some other bad shots, that ought to be the only stroke that will cost. I might still be able to make a par if I hit my fourth shot close to the pin and hole the putt.

The key is to honestly assess your ability to pull off that career shot. Ask yourself, how many times out of 10 can I hit the ball through that small opening? Remember, you are always playing with your average shot, not your best shot.

In the Wind, Don't Get Fancy, Just Allow for It

Bobby Jones once said that wind adds or subtracts yardage to the hole. In other words, if you are shooting into the wind, it adds yardage. If you are shooting with the wind, it subtracts yardage. Playing in crosswinds gets a little tricky because that depends on your ball-flight tendencies. Whether you use the wind or resist it hinges on your skill and the requirements of the shot. Generally, however, you are better off allowing for the wind than trying to resist it.

Always remember: Into the wind, the curvature of the ball is exaggerated. A gentle draw can become a hook and a soft fade can become a slice, so allow for it. The opposite is true when the wind is behind you. It is difficult to curve the ball downwind, so unless you have to, it might be better not to try.

Some teachers and players advocate teeing the ball lower into the wind, but I don't. I like to see your swing shape and swing pace the same as on a calm day, and teeing the ball the normal height will help you do that. Teeing the ball lower, especially for higher handicappers, only causes you to subconsciously hit down on the ball, which in turn pops it up. That's the last thing you want when it's windy. Just leave the tee in the ground to promote solid contact. And avoid trying to hit the ball any harder than normal.

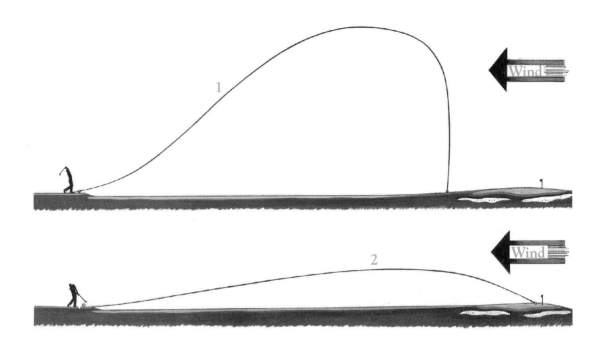

Into the Wind, Take Too Much Club and Swing Easy

The worst thing you can do into the wind is try to hit the ball harder. That only puts more spin on the ball, causing it to upshoot and actually go shorter (1). Instead, take more club and swing easier, so the ball doesn't have as much spin (2). Into the wind a good rule of thumb is to have a club in your hand that you are concerned about hitting too far.

Downwind, Drive with a Higher-lofted Club

On approach shots downwind, you still don't want to hit the ball as hard because it will tend to sail on you. From the tee, almost without exception, you will drive the ball farther with a fairway wood than with the driver. Even highly skilled tour players, when they want optimum distance downwind, drive the ball with a 3-wood rather than with a driver. Why? Because the ball spins more off a 3-wood's loft, goes higher and rides the wind better (A). A driver shot going downwind doesn't have enough spin to keep the ball airborne as long (B). It's like trying to take an airplane off with the wind. Pilots take off into the wind to get better lift.

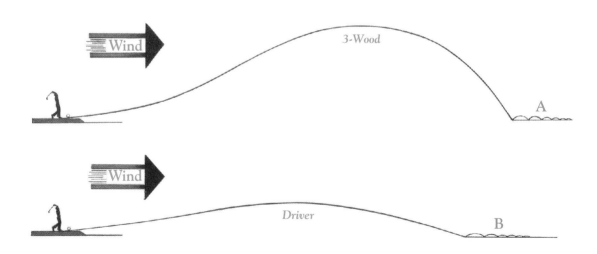

Addendum: | Putting It All Together

Most of the mistakes I see players make in strategy come from panic, or anxiety, or impatience—the feeling that they need to recover from a bad shot on the very next one. But that may not be the opportunity. The opportunity to get that stroke back may come two or three holes later. Be patient.

Never take the risk of losing a shot unless there is potential for gaining a shot. You always need to keep the risk-reward ratio reasonable. For instance, on an advancement shot, on either a par 5 or a long par 4, you would never want to hit a club that you are uncomfortable with just to hit a shorter club into the green. Keep in mind the 1-to-1 ratio.

Visualization

We talked earlier about image transfer. If you can learn to transfer an image that is familiar to you, that you are comfortable shooting at and that you have had some success shooting at, it can give you an elevated level of confidence on the course. It can help you avoid thoughts of mechanics while you're playing. Maybe your image is a target you often shoot at on your practice range. Whatever it is, try visualizing it on the course.

Stick to Your Routines

Your routines on the course are invaluable and they have to be practiced to the point that they become natural habits that require no thought. They are extremely important when things are not going well. And you have to make a commitment to stay with them regardless of what happens. Go through your shot routine every time, *every* time. Do it religiously.

Dealing with Pressure

Say you are playing a four-man nassau. The match comes down to the 18th hole, there are two presses on the line, your partner is already in his pocket, and you have a five-foot putt to tie. Obviously, there is more pressure on you. Or is there? It depends on how you look at it. You need to understand what you can and cannot do. Let's say you are a player whose putting skills allow you to make 60 percent of your five-foot putts on the course. The reality of the game is that you are going to be successful only some of the time. Tell yourself this and then try your best. Then accept whatever happens.

Ed Sneed and Hubert Green have both missed putts inside of three feet on the 18th green that would have won or tied for the Masters Tournament. Some would say they weren't tough enough. But I don't think it has anything to do with that. I feel those were just unfortunate occasions when one of the putts that is on the percentage-of-miss side happened to them at inopportune times.

Playing Well When It Counts

Some people play well in practice, but then don't play as well when in competition. If your practice rounds are good enough, you need to learn to play your practice-round game when it counts. Tom Watson says he learned not to choke. What that means is he learned not to get in his own way by making it too important. For a large majority of people in those circumstances, the more they try the more they grind, and the more serious they get the worse they perform. Watson had to find ways to not make the outcome unreasonably important, and he did, mostly by getting himself in position to win enough times that he finally became comfortable in that situation. Give yourself the best chance to be successful, then have the courage to live with the outcome.

Giving yourself the best chance to be successful means different things to different people, depending on their personalities and their tendencies. For example, an unfocused person, a casual person, a person who has a tendency to not try hard enough needs to try harder. A person who tends to be too serious, to overthink, to try too hard needs to try less.

So you need to understand yourself and to understand what characteristics really give you the best chance to be successful. Sport psychologist Dr. Bob Rotella says, "Golf is a game of mistakes played by imperfect humans." In pressure situations you are probably going to fail more times than you succeed. That's reality. So you need to have a short-term memory for your failures, and a long-term memory for your successes.

Senior tour player Jim Colbert, after making two double-bogeys in a row in the final round of the 1992 Bruno's Classic in Birmingham, said, "If you play a sport long enough, you are going to have all kinds of opportunities to embarrass yourself." Golf is a sport. Pressure comes with the territory. So enjoy it and appreciate it as a part of the game.

Be Sure to Have Fun

To truly get the most out of this game, you have to ask yourself, "Why am I playing?" Having fun to me means shooting low scores. So if I am giving myself the best chance I can to shoot a low score, I am having fun. Be realistic about the goals you set, the things you try to accomplish. A lot of people don't have fun because they have unrealistic expectations. For example, I have an acquaintance who has not been playing golf very long. He has had some instruction, but not from me. If I put him 50 yards from the green in the center of the fairway and gave him his pitching wedge or his 9-iron, he would not be able to hit the ball on the green half the time. And he recently told me, "I have just got to find a driver I can hit from the tee." If you have a golf stroke that won't hit the ball on the green from 50 yards half the time, there is no driver that you can hit from the tee with any reasonable degree of success!

Unfortunately, my friend's attitude is not uncommon. A lot of people set themselves up for failure because they are totally unrealistic about what they expect from themselves. Understand your limitations, and enjoy your strengths. Work on your weaknesses, but don't expect them to disappear quickly.

They will evaporate more quickly and permanently, however, if you approach the game in the manner outlined in this book. Be specific in terms of the three different areas—the Golf Swing, the Golf Shot and the Golf Score. Don't mix them. Do your job in each of the Three Games of Golf, and you will find genuine happiness and enjoyment and a true appreciation for the greatest game of all.